THE RESURRECTION...

It's Breathtaking

**A daily journey from
Ash Wednesday to Easter**

K.L. KANDEL

ISBN-13: 978-0615977478

Unless otherwise identified, all Scripture quotations
in this publication are taken from the Holy Bible:
New International Version. (2011). Grand Rapids,
Mich.: Zondervan. Used by permission; and the
King James Version (KJV).

About K.L. Kandel

K.L. Kandel is the pen name for Kris Kandel Schwambach, Karen Kandel Kizlin, Kathie Kandel Poe and Linda Kandel Mason, four sisters with some very different life experiences.

As mothers, grandmothers, teachers, and Bible teachers, their writing reveals a sense of wonder, discovery and a heart to connect with the hearts and homes of those around them.

Learn more, explore additional writings, and contact K.L. Kandel at **www.klkandel.com**.

Also By K.L. Kandel

Take A Deep Breath... It's Christmas
A 40 Day Journey Towards The Heart Of Christmas

Catch Your Breath... It's A New Beginning
A 40 Day Journey Towards A New Year,
A New Season Or A New Start

Learn more at **www.klkandel.com**.

Special Thanks

Perhaps you've heard the adage, *"You can't judge a book by its cover."* Well, the covers on our books are so beautiful that we hope you will judge ours.

Jeremy Secrest, my son-in-law, takes our manuscript and brings such wonderful design to it. We are thrilled with the layout, the font, the color choices because he has an artist's eye.

You can read Jeremy's book, *Creative You*, available on Amazon.

Thank you for all your hard work on the books. You are a great blessing. (Thanks also for the grandchildren you and Joy have given to John and me, you really won't be able to top that.)

Love,

Mom and the Aunts

We would also like to express our appreciation to the people in positions of leadership and government who gave us days off work so we could have time to write this book. We're talking about those who called off school with snow days and delays this winter. It gave us extra hours to write and for that we want to offer our gratitude. You didn't know you were accommodating our schedule but we wanted to say *"Thanks"* anyway. And now that we're done with the book, we don't need any more snow days... we have vacations planned in June!

K. L. Kandel

Dedication

It is our desire to dedicate everything we do to Jesus. He is the author and perfecter of our faith. So, with grateful hearts, we dedicate this book to our Lord and Savior, Jesus Christ. Thank you.

Table Of Contents

Introduction

You may notice that we like to write.

We especially like to write about life's ordinary moments and use them to point to the extraordinary.

You may also notice that we like to tell stories.

We're going to ask you to step onto the rug. Now get ready, we're going to yank it out from under you. You might want to set your coffee down for this.

You've picked up an Easter book...

Twas the Night before Christmas and four little girls were not nestled all snug in their beds.

Christmas Eve was the longest night of the year. After a midnight church service we went to bed and we did fall asleep. But falling asleep and staying asleep are two different things. As soon as one of us would wake up, we were all up because whispered through our bedroom in hushed tones were the words, *"Are you awake?"* We thought we could hear the gifts shouting at us from beneath the tree and just in case the Grinch was real and he might come to steal them, we needed to be up to get them opened. We went to our mom and dad's room for the traditional 2:00 AM wake up call. And we received the traditional answer, *"Not yet, go back to bed."*

We needed reinforcements, so we went to see if our brothers were awake. We thought Bill, being the youngest and so very cute, could be our secret weapon. We assumed our parents couldn't turn him down. But alas, they did. We also didn't think it was fair for us to have all the fun watching the seconds tick by on the old alarm clock in our room.

So how do you kill the hours between 2:00 AM and the time we were finally allowed to be up?
You create an imaginary world of whimsical, nonsensical, hysterical, comical stories. Super Dan and his trusty sidekick Willie Clause, AKA Willnut (not their real names) were born at the Christmas season. They could fly, could lift Grandma's gigantic, enormous, bovinical bull (not the bull's real name) with one finger, and leap tall buildings with a single bound. So if you are reading this and you know one of our brothers, please don't reveal their secret identities. There is more super hero work to be done, more tall buildings to leap over (Although at this point in their lives, they might have to crawl under or else slam into them.) and more bulls to be lifted, oh wait, that's *"bull markets"* to be lifted.

And so we became storytellers.

Every life is made up of a series of stories that can become parables. Even if the rug gets yanked beneath you, remember it just might be a story that becomes a parable. Parables teach.

We are inviting you to enter the mundane with us. Take a few moments and look around at the simple little stories of life and visit the lesson.

But don't stay very long looking at our faces. It isn't ours we want you to remember. We are going to step forward to tell the story but then hopefully step back into the shadows so you can look into the Face of the Real Story.

Every life carries a message.

We speak it.
We live it.
Because He spoke it.
He lived it.
It whispers.
It shouts.
Let's listen.

By the way, it was one of Jesus' favorite ways to teach…it still is.

So why would we start an Easter book with a Christmas story? Because the Bible is all one story, His Story. The resurrection was birthed in the heart of God before the creation of the world. God promised it to Adam and Eve in the garden when He said that the seed of the woman would crush the head of the serpent. The prophets foretold it, the Scripture revealed it, and Jesus fulfilled it.

Now feel free to pick your coffee back up and let's get ready.

Preface

Fat Tuesday...terrible name. Maybe you call it Mardi Gras. Let's just take these words apart. Mardi is French for Tuesday. Gras is French for fat. Yep, there it is, Fat Tuesday.

Ash Wednesday...somber name. Sackcloth and ashes are signs for mourning and fasting.

These two days stand side-by-side vying for attention forty-six days before Easter. Fat Tuesday, for some, means that you eat-up, drink-up, fill-up.

Ash Wednesday often means that you then throw-up, give-up, fess-up.

So what is up with these days?

Let's take a journey up to the single most defining moment in all of history: the resurrection of Jesus Christ.

It is a look back, a look inside and a look forward.

You don't need to spend very long in the pages of this little book called a devotional, but hopefully it will cause you to want to spend more time in the pages of The Book that calls us to devotion.

Every day between now and Resurrection Sunday, we are going to open God's Word.

Each day will be a chance to explore. The weekdays are to investigate and Sundays are to celebrate.

For six days we will call you to be a student. On the seventh day we will call you to be a worshiper.

What we will discover is that in one single moment the grave was split open, time was split apart and eternity split in two.

The Resurrection...It's Breathtaking
A daily journey from Ash Wednesday to Easter

Day 1

Clothes make the man.

You are what you eat.

I'm not sure John the Baptist would agree. The Bible tells us he wore camel's hair with a leather belt. Now let's look at that. It was not velvety soft lamb's wool. It was not downy alpaca yarn. It was camel's hair, scratchy and coarse. He ate locusts and wild honey. When it says locusts, do you know what that is? Yep, the grasshopper family. So how would John the Baptist have felt about the two statements? I think he would have said, *"Ahhhh, I don't care."*

But for us, we do care...sometimes too much. We spend a great deal of time thinking about clothing and food. I admit in my career, I do try to dress for success. Sometimes I manage the right outfit for the job. Sometimes I get it WAY wrong.

I have taught every grade level from pre-kindergarten to high school. I have tried to match what I was wearing to what I needed for the day. One day I was going to be doing interviews. I decided that I needed to look very professional, since people coming for the prospective jobs would be dressed up. I chose a tailored look. I had recently purchased a black skirt that had a green fern pattern. I had a black sweater with just a bit of that same green ribbed at the neck along with a matching green jacket. I looked at myself. Yes, this would do. I was looking fine.

There were two of us on the team who were doing the interviews. He was the twenty-something young, junior high teacher and I was the veteran (Isn't that a nice way to say old?) high school teacher.

We interviewed the first candidate. I think I scared her off, so she left quickly, leaving us some time before our next interview. My co-worker looked at me with a very strange look on his face.

"Kathie, where did you get that skirt?"

I was stunned. I couldn't fathom why a young man would remotely need that information, so I joked. *"What? Why do you care?"* After all I knew I was looking pretty fine.

He was dead serious and again asked. *"Where did you get that skirt?"*

I could see that he wasn't kidding so I gave him the name of the shop.

"Ummm, Kathie, those are marijuana leaves on the skirt."

I want you to understand, I went to college in the late sixties-early seventies. But drugs were never on my agenda for life. I never smoked marijuana (or even smoked it and failed to inhale). I never tried cocaine or LSD or any of the other offerings that called people to experiment. I never thought I was too smart anyway, so burning up or destroying brain cells seemed like a poor idea to me. I had no frame of reference when it came to drugs, yet I was sure that he was wrong.

I looked down at my skirt. *"NO THEY AREN'T!"* My voice rose to a fevered pitch.

"Kathie, before I came here to teach I used to teach drug awareness at the police academy. Those are marijuana leaves."

Suddenly I went from cool, collected and professional to sweating profusely and wilting. I bolted from the interview room. I ran down the hall straight to the principal's office. I did not stop at the secretary's desk to ask if he was busy. I did not pause at the counselor's desk to chat. I barged right into the principal's office with my co-worker right behind me, who was by this time laughing so hard he could barely walk. I saw nothing funny about this. I closed both doors to the office and made my way to the side of the desk so my boss could get a full view of the skirt. I looked at him and with sheer panic in my voice, I asked, *"What do you think about my skirt?"*

Now in retrospect this was not even remotely a fair question. Here I was a woman asking fashion advice from my male boss.

He stuttered. *"Uuummm, it's nice?"*

Really, what was he supposed to say?

I said, *"No, look at my skirt. Are these marijuana leaves?"*

He kind of cocked his head to scrutinize. His only response was, *"Weeeeellllll?"*

That was enough for me. I was frantic, *"What do you want me to do?"*

This was a public high school. Teachers are not really supposed to wear drug related clothing. But I also live fifteen miles from the school. *"Do you want me to go home and change clothes?"*

This would at best have taken me an hour.

He thought about that for a bit. *"No, just turn your skirt inside out."*

Turn the skirt inside out? TURN THE SKIRT INSIDE OUT! This was a solution for kids who wore T-shirts that might say something that was not appropriate for a high school. If someone was walking around with inside out clothing, it spoke a message that I did not want to speak.

"I am not turning my skirt inside out!" I knew this was bordering on insubordination, but honestly I was upset.

Was the principal upset? By this time both my co-worker and my principal were almost beside themselves, doubled over, having a hard time breathing. I, again, found nothing funny about the situation.

Finally my boss managed to cough out, *"Kathie, just go hang out in your room behind the desk. Stay there until the end of the day and have people come to you."*

Did this end the conversation of the marijuana skirt? Was this kept confidential, quiet and discreet? OHHHH NOOOO. Throughout the day I received emails from teachers around the building showing me pictures of marijuana in different settings and from different camera angles. Teachers came by just to *"chat"*, so they could see this very conservative teacher be a walking billboard for drugs. It was one of the longest school days on record.

When I was sure the halls were cleared for the day, I slinked out by a back door.

John the Baptist wore camel's hair...that was looking like a better choice all the time.

Luke 1, Malachi 4, John 3

Behind the scenes, it's the place where much of
the work is accomplished, but little of the applause
ever reaches. It often feels thankless, tiresome and
tedious. It is coming in for the set-up, the back-up,
the clean-up but rarely does it mean that your name
is up in lights.

It is where most of us will spend most of our
Christian lives. But we're in good company.

It is where John the Baptist lived.

His ministry began even before anyone ever saw his
face. He started his job in the shadows.

His parents, Zechariah and Elizabeth, were way too
old to have a child. They were well beyond the years
of child bearing. Their youthfulness had dried up.
Their skin was wrinkled. Their once lovely hands
showed those telltale signs of age, brown ugly spots,
veins too close to the surface. They had hoped and
prayed that those hands would soothe a child, their
arms would cradle a baby, their ears would hear
their own baby's coos and giggles, but month after
month that door was constantly closed. And now
it was permanently closed. They were not to be
blessed with a baby.

But God is bigger than closed doors. God is bigger

than aged bodies. God is bigger than impossible and sure enough there was a child, a miracle to alert the world that the Savior was coming.

Even before his birth, John began his ministry when Mary, carrying her own unborn child, arrived for a visit. Hidden behind the walls of his mother's womb, John leaped. He jumped for joy that he was in the presence of the Savior. He alerted his mother outside with a kick of his heels inside. The world couldn't see, but Elizabeth knew.

John knew he wasn't the main event. He knew it was his job to be the set-up crew. He knew he was there to point others to the One who would come after him.

He was a fulfillment of Scripture. His coming had been foretold.

"See, I will send the prophet Elijah to you before that great and dreadful day of the Lord comes. He will turn the hearts of the parents to their children, and the hearts of the children to their parents; or else I will come and strike the land with total destruction." Malachi 4:5

Wait a minute, this says Elijah would come. But Jesus Himself identified John as this fulfillment.

Read Matthew 11:14 and Mark 9:13.

John's birth had been announced by the angel Gabriel. His birth had been foretold. His very life was a fulfillment of the Scripture. That might have brought a star mentality to some, but not to John. He was good to be the voice to call people to the Savior.

He didn't get hurt if people didn't like his clothes, or his food choices. The man ate locusts, bugs that go hop in the night. Of course he added just a dash of wild honey. Yum. I do have to wonder if he cooked those babies to a crackling crispness. (Feel free to call Kris or Linda for this recipe. They claim to have perfected the art of cooking to just the right amount of dryness.) But hey, locusts were prevalent and whenever he felt a little peckish, all he need do was reach down and dig in.

John didn't get upset if someone didn't know his name, because it was not in the least about him. It was absolutely about Jesus.

Listen to John's own words in John 3:30, *"He must become greater; I must become less."*

John knew his mission. John knew his place. His whole job was to let his life point to Jesus, to let his words call people to be ready to meet the Savior. His task was to lift up Jesus so all could come to Him.

But isn't that where our lives are to be as well, pointing people to the Messiah? No matter what we do, we are not the main event. Our job is to know Him, and to make Him known. Sometimes that means breezing in with a pot of soup. Sometimes it means speaking before thousands. Sometimes it's cleaning a bathroom when no one is looking. Sometimes it's up front when everyone is looking. Sometimes it's eating gourmet; sometimes it's eating bugs. Sometimes it feels little, but then it turns out big.

His job...be the voice. Our job...be the hands, the feet, the presence of the Savior. What little big thing will happen today?

Day 2

Baptisms are big. They are significant. They mark that someone has passed from death to life, that a miracle has taken place. They are huge, important moments in the church and life changing moments for the person. Baptisms should be celebrated. They should be memorable.

The pastor was new to pastoring. He was new to the church. This was one of his first times to baptize and of course he wanted to do it right. His hands might have been a little sweaty, but no matter, they would be wet in a few moments. His voice a little shaky, perhaps no one would notice, but if they did, it could be attributed to the emotion of the moment. He wanted this to be memorable.

And so he began. He leaned the man back in the water. That went well; at least he didn't drop him. An awesome event in this new believer's life, the pastor started to speak, but then... suddenly...nothing. He could not remember what it was he was supposed to say. He started again, but nothing.

It's called audience amnesia. It happens. The brain falls out of your head onto the floor and what's left is wide-open, empty space. All that you wanted to say somehow slips away into the fog and there's nothing. It's bad timing to have your brain fall out of your head when you are trying to speak in front of a group. It is worse timing when your brain falls into the baptistery and someone is down there to greet it.

He pondered. He thought. No, it wasn't coming. He tried, but as the moments passed, the longer it went, the more he couldn't remember.

As the seconds ticked by the audience started to hold their breath. What was this new pastor doing? Baptisms never took this long. Anyone waiting in the wings next to be baptized might have been second guessing that decision, having to hold your breath for that long. Perhaps the better part of wisdom would be to wait for another day with a different pastor.

Then, maybe it was the writhing and kicking under the water that brought him out of his stupor, but the pastor finally remembered and brought the man up out of the water, sputtering and gasping for air. The congregation collectively exhaled.

Baptisms should be memorable. It was.

Wet suit and oxygen tank aren't normally required.

Matthew 3

John preached. It is what he did. John baptized. It is what he did.

People came because he spoke about hope for a new life. His message was of repentance. Turn from wickedness and sin and find forgiveness.

Matthew 3:11, *"I baptize you with water for repentance. But after me comes one who is more powerful than I, whose sandals I am not worthy to carry. He will baptize you with the Holy Spirit and fire. His winnowing fork is in His hand, and He will clear His threshing floor, gathering His wheat into His barn and burning up the chaff with unquenchable fire."*

His was an incredibly powerful message calling for repentance and many came. People from all walks of life came to hear. They listened to his words of hope for a new beginning. Any who came confessing their sins, anyone who came seeking forgiveness from Almighty God, found it. It was available for all.

They listened, repented and then were baptized. The baptism was an outward sign of a new beginning.

And then suddenly, Jesus came to be baptized too. John knew that with Jesus the tables were turned. He did not need to baptize Jesus. Jesus needed to baptize him.

Matthew 3:14-15, *"John tried to deter Him, saying, 'I need to be baptized by You, and do You come to me?'*

Jesus replied, 'Let it be so now; it is proper for us to do this to fulfill all righteousness.' Then John consented."

So right there in the Jordan River, John the Baptist baptized the Savior of the world. John obeyed the Lord's request to fulfill all righteousness, and the Lord showed us the importance of baptism.

And then suddenly, a miracle, heaven opened and the Spirit of God, like a dove, settled down on Jesus. The Spirit of God was hovering just as at the creation of the world.

Verse 17: *"And a voice from heaven said, 'This is my Son, whom I love; with Him I am well pleased.'"*

Day 3

The lid to the cookie jar was askew. There she stood on a chair. Crumbs were dropping behind her, because her little clasped hands were trying to conceal the evidence.

Her daddy saw her and immediately questioned, *"Kristie, did you get a cookie?"*

Temptation...even though she was little, she knew she was not supposed to get into the cookie jar. But hunger, coupled with the idea of a cookie before dinner, the cookie jar there on the counter, the chair scooted to just the right place to reach it, Mommy and Daddy in the other room...the temptation proved too much. Those delicious cookies in that forbidden cookie jar called too loudly and the voice of the evil one spoke ever so softly. So like every single one of us has, since Eve ate the fruit, she listened.

"Did you get a cookie?" Now her dad already knew the answer. He could see exactly what had happened. But he wanted her to be honest, to own up to her sin.

But here she was, now confronted with yet another temptation.

What should she say?

She was young, not yet old enough to understand theology, or the good versus evil concept. Her parents had worked to teach her, even though she was little, to tell the truth. She knew what truth meant.

But no one had to teach her to lie.

As parents and grandparents we have to teach our children to do what is right. Teaching them to always tell the truth is vital. But no one ever has to teach a child to lie. They can get that all on their own. Why? Because we are born sinners and we sin. It comes naturally. It is the reason why we so desperately need a Savior.

So how did she answer this question about getting the cookie?

She said, *"No."*

NO? There she stood with the cookie in her hands and yet she was telling him she did not get a cookie from that jar.

Okay, again she was little. She was hoping beyond hope to get away with it. She didn't. But when we are tempted and we sin, how often do we say that we haven't done it? We cover it over, explain it away, hide it behind our backs, and deny it.

I know because I've done the same thing. When confronted with temptation we have opened the cookie jar, taken what we should not have taken, spoken words of hatred, or gossip, or malice, or lies, said what we should not say, done what we should not do, gone where we should not go.

We hope beyond hope that we can get away with it.

We cannot. It is why we are in desperate need of a Savior.

Every man, woman and child on the planet, when confronted with temptation has sinned...except for One.

Matthew 4

Matthew 4:1 tells us *"Then Jesus was led by the Spirit into the wilderness to be tempted by the devil."*

Let me clarify. The temptation itself is not sin. It is when we yield to the temptation that we have sinned.

Jesus was tempted. He went into the wilderness tempted by the devil. He had gone for forty days without food. That's a really long time not to eat. But for forty days and nights He had dined with the Father, feasting on God's presence. (Doesn't that sound like a lovely experience?) Jesus was spiritually prepared, but after forty days He would have been physically weak, bordering on starvation.

When satan told Jesus to turn the stones into bread, that would have been an unbelievable temptation. Every cell, every fiber of His being would have been crying out for food.

And how did He respond to the temptation? *"Jesus answered, 'It is written: Man shall not live on bread alone, but on every word that comes from the mouth of God.'"* Matthew 4:4

Satan tried again, questioning who Jesus was and challenging Him to prove He was the Son of God. Jesus once again came back with the Word. *"It is also written: Do not put the Lord your God to the test.*" Matthew 4:7

One last time Matthew tells us that satan came and this time he took Jesus up to the high mountains. He showed Him all of the kingdoms of the world. Satan offered these to Jesus and the only thing He had to do was bow down to worship the devil.

I love how Jesus answered this, *"Away from me satan! For it is written: 'Worship the Lord your God, and serve Him only.'"* Matthew 4:10

It is the response we should have when we feel tempted... *"Away from me satan!"*

Jesus never sinned. So how did He fight the temptation?

He fasted. He spent time in prayer and fellowship with God. He knew the Word.

Hmmm, seems like a good pattern for us.

Day 4

She was so hurt from the betrayal. She begged her dad to stay, to do what was right. He wasn't listening. He was leaving. She wrapped her arms around him, pleading, *"Daddy, please don't go. If you love me, you will stay."* But he did leave. He wrenched himself free from her grasp and walked away. With his actions, he also left a huge tear in her heart.

She wasn't a little girl. She was turning twenty-one soon, but when a daddy leaves, it puts a child right back into childhood and the heart is just as broken as if she had been five.

An emptiness in her heart, a hole that desperately needed to be filled, she began to search for something, someone to fill the void.

When we have such a void in our hearts, we need to run to Jesus and allow Him to fill the space. The Bible is always a model for us. In John 2, when at the marriage in Cana the wine jars were empty, Mary went to Jesus and asked Him to fill them. He did, and filled them with the most marvelous wine they had ever tasted. His filling is always so much better than anything we can come up with.

But often our pain is so big and our judgment is so skewed, that we search in the wrong places.

She found someone.

I am going to call him N.M.R. These initials are not his real initials but, in reality, they fit.

He went to church. Going to church is good. But it doesn't make someone a Christian. It makes them a churchgoer. He followed her around like a puppy. As a mom I could almost not stand this. I wanted someone with backbone and initiative. I didn't see either of those in N.M.R. I mentioned that to Julie. Maybe I mentioned it a few times, well, okay, maybe a few more than a few. I wanted to make sure she got the message.

He did seem, though, to be completely committed to her. That came across as good except that he appeared to be hanging onto the coat tails of her involvement in spiritual things. I may have mentioned that to Julie a time or two as well.

What also wasn't good was the anger that lived behind his eyes. It showed up sometimes when things didn't go exactly the way he wanted them to go. It showed up when a competition broke out and he didn't emerge the winner. It showed up toward me, the mother, because he could tell I was not on board with the relationship.

I might have casually mentioned that to Julie on a couple of occasions, you know, just in case she wasn't aware of it.

I could clearly see that this relationship was NOT ANY GOOD. So I came up with a game plan to try to help Julie see that. I used those words as my inspiration. I named my strategy N.A.G.

I talked, preached, complained, talked more, preached more, complained more and very clearly, in my sweet, motherly way, explained why this young man was wrong for her. I pointed out all of the flaws. Yes, I was sure that the NAG plan was the way to go.

And how did that work out?

The more I spoke, the deeper Julie dug her heels in. You see, she had to come up with reasons why he was NOT a bad choice. She began to find every good thing about N.M.R. and to explain those to me, to convince me.

Finally I stopped talking to Julie about him. I could see that it was making her more committed. She was convincing herself that he was a right choice. I was so afraid she would convince herself right into an engagement, a marriage.

Instead, I began to pray. Each morning I went in and sat next to Julie.

Part of my prayer went something like this...

"Dear Jesus, I know that You see this relationship. I know that this is not the man that You have for

Julie. Would You please bring Your choice to her....”

Sometimes, she would interrupt. *“Mom...”*

I would pat her and interrupt back, *“Julie, I'm not talking to you, I'm talking to Jesus.”* and then I would go on with my prayer.

“Lord, please bring a man into her life who loves You with His whole heart, a man who will follow You and will lead her and their family...”

And each day I prayed that way...until a few weeks later some happy news, *“Mom, I'm not seeing N. M. R. anymore.”* (Did you get that? Not Mr. Right!)

There had been another young man in her life. He was her very dear friend. He was her trusted confidant through all the strife, through even some dating catastrophes. He challenged her to pray. He guided her to the right because he loved the Lord.

On December 8, 2001, I.M.R. (not his real initials but stands for Is Mr. Right) became her husband and my bedside prayers were answered for a young man who was fully committed to Christ.

He still is and so is she.

John 2

It was a Tuesday, a great day for a wedding. You see way back in the beginning on that third day of creation there was a double blessing. You can read about that in Genesis 1:9-13. Because God said twice on that day that it was good, Tuesday was considered a great day for a marriage.

Jesus, His mother, and His disciples were all there when Jesus' mother noticed something. She observed that they had run out of wine.

Today if we run out of refreshments at a reception, we might say, *"Listen, I never promised to meet all your needs, so there's a great place down the road where you can get food really fast."*

But during the time of Christ it would have been terrible for the family to have the stigma of running out of wine. Mary saw this and knew exactly what to do. She went to Jesus. (I think it is wonderful that God gives parents the ability to notice things, so we can take them to Jesus.)

She merely stated in John 2:3, *"They have no more wine."* That was it. So simple and yet in verse five we know she had that calm assurance that Jesus was going to answer. She said to the servants, *"Do whatever He tells you."*

Standing right there were six stone water jars which were used for ceremonial washing. Each of them held from twenty to thirty gallons of water. The servants went to Jesus and then did exactly what He told them to do. They instantly obeyed. They didn't question. They filled those jars to the brim. There was no room for anything else. Suddenly, there was an abundance of wine.

At that wedding, once again, the Creator of the universe spoke and six jars were filled with the most wonderful, flawless wine any of them had ever tasted. It was more than enough. It was more than amazing. It was miraculous.

So for us, when we are empty, when we have had pain, or disappointment, or trials that have left us with a hole in our heart, here is a picture of what we need to do. Go to Jesus. Do what He says and let Him fill us. His filling is miraculous.

Day 5

Celebration Day

Psalm 144

"Praise be to the Lord my rock..."

As you read Psalm 144 today, celebrate who God is.

Day 6

She was not quite three. Her parents didn't even know that she knew the phrase. They later guessed that she had either heard them say it at home, or maybe she had heard it at church. But they were completely shocked when Great Aunt Olive and Great Uncle Dave came to visit and this child asked a very adult question.

It was the first time the children had met these relatives, so her dad introduced her to this new aunt and uncle. She at first couldn't believe it, and made that clear, *"You're not my Uncle Dave."* You see she had another uncle by that name and this man did not remotely look like him. But she then understood this was a new uncle, one she had not met before.

Uncle Dave knelt down next to this little girl so he could get eye to eye with her. She looked directly at him.

She asked, *"Uncle Dave, are you born again?"*

"Born again?" An interesting question coming from such a tiny child. Uncle Dave laughed nervously, *"Oh, isn't that cute?"*

But he didn't answer the question.

The visit went on, everyone enjoyed the day, and soon it came time for Uncle Dave and Aunt Olive to travel the one hundred miles back to their home.

But was the question forgotten?

No, it was not.

Uncle Dave went back home and could not get past the question, *"Uncle Dave, are you born again?"* He understood what she was asking. He had been to church, was married to a preacher's daughter, but Uncle Dave hadn't put much thought into his own salvation until this tiny child asked him face to face. It kept ringing in his ears. He kept wrestling with it.

Sunday came and he knew what he had to do. He went to church and when the pastor invited people to ask Jesus to be their Savior, Uncle Dave did.

Now he could answer the question.

"Uncle Dave, are you born again?"

a resounding..."*Yes!*"

John 3

Nicodemus was a Pharisee, a member of the ruling council. I've wondered if perhaps he could have been sitting there in the temple courts years before, amazed as a twelve year old boy was questioning and answering the leaders.

We don't know what initially prompted Nicodemus to want to meet with Jesus by night. But what we do know is that he wanted an answer to an unasked question. So he went to the One who has all the answers.

"Rabbi, we know that you are a teacher who has come from God. For no one could perform the signs you are doing if God were not with him." John 3:2

Jesus could see right into the very heart of Nicodemus and told him what he needed to know. *"Very truly I tell you, no one can see the kingdom of God unless they are born again."* John 3:3

Nicodemus was confused. That was not a phrase he had heard before. It had not been tossed around at political rallies or used in the synagogue or the temple. It seemed illogical. How could that be? How could someone be born again?

But even though maybe we've heard that phrase

'born again' lots of times, even though for us it's been around for two thousand years, people still are not quite sure what it means. Some think that being good enough is somehow a ticket to heaven. *"If the good outweighs the bad on the grand scale of life, then I will get in."*

But here's the truth, we can never, ever, ever be good enough to get to heaven.

Nicodemus is an example of that. When we look at him, we have to say that most likely he was a keeper of the law. He was a Pharisee. He loved the law and worked to obey it. Was it enough? It was not! He could not be good enough.

We can't be good enough either. Why? Because we are all sinners. We are stained with sin and being good does not take it away.

"Jesus answered, 'Very truly I tell you, no one can enter the kingdom of God unless they are born of water and the Spirit. Flesh gives birth to flesh, but the Spirit gives birth to spirit. You should not be surprised at my saying, 'You must be born again.'"
John 3:5-7

So there has to be a rebirth. It had to happen for Nicodemus and it has to happen for us. We, like Nicodemus, have to come to Christ. We have to acknowledge that we are sinners. We have to ask

Him for forgiveness and look to Him as our Savior, the only One who can clean our sin stained lives. It is the only way to be reborn.

Did Nicodemus get it? Yes, and we know that he did, because he was the one, along with Joseph of Arimathea, to bury Jesus. He was a follower of the Savior.

So what about you? Do you know that you have been *'born again'*? Do you know that you have looked to the One who was lifted up on a cross to die for YOU, so that your sins could be forgiven, completely taken away?

If not, you can do that today, right here, right now. Romans 10:13 says *"Everyone who calls on the Name of the Lord will be saved."*

Start with a simple prayer:

Dear Jesus,

I know the Bible says that I am a sinner. I am sorry for my sins and ask You to come into my life to forgive me of my sins and make me Your child. I accept you as my Lord, my Savior and my very best Friend.

Thank You for dying for me. Help me to live for You.

Thank You. In Jesus' name I pray.

Amen

"For God so loved the world that He gave His one and only Son, that whoever believes in Him shall not perish but have eternal life." John 3:16

Day 7

"It's cancer."

I had to wonder if I had heard him right, the doctor said it so nonchalantly, like it was yesterday's news. Of course he was used to delivering this information, he was an oncologist, but we were by no means used to hearing it. The last immediate family member to have this diagnosis was my dad and his cancer was terminal. My husband was now my father's exact age when Dad was diagnosed, and it was the exact same kind of cancer. And I was the exact same age as my mother when she became a widow.

Cancer! Cancer is one of those over the cliff kinds of diagnoses. It speaks fear and more fear and a million questions and begs an answer to one of the over-arching questions of *"Now what?"* But the *"Now what?"* was answered...surgery, and right away. It did not matter what our schedule was. It did not matter if we had work or vacation plans. Our plans for the next little while or perhaps a long while were off the burner.

Cancer! The rug under us was pulled and we were having a little trouble standing. We were having a little trouble breathing.

But when we start to fall, when our strength fails, when the air is knocked out of us, the Lord rushes in with His big arms to catch us, hold us, cradle us and give us His breath.

I went to the place where I could find strength. I opened my Bible. I turned to Genesis 26.

I want to interject something. The Bible is an amazing Book. It's deeper than we can ever begin to imagine. And God meets us in its pages. I absolutely believe that God can use any passage at any time to speak a word to our hearts.

I read verses 16-22. Now this is one of those texts in the Bible that we might skip. It feels at first glance that it's just there to progress us to the next part of the story. It's probably not a text someone might choose to teach about, unless they were teaching through the Bible, and then most likely just a nod to it. But for me it has become a miracle passage.

This Scripture is about Isaac and some squabbles with the Philistines over wells in the land. Water is absolutely necessary for life but Israel is a desert climate. You dig to find the water. Isaac and his servants kept finding wells but each time there seemed to be a problem. But right here, with a mostly overlooked section of Scripture, the Words jumped off the page. God spoke to my heart, *"Do you see? Everywhere Isaac went there was a problem. But everywhere he went, he found fresh water. There may be some difficulties in the days ahead, but I will give you Living Water."* It was a promise to me. The Almighty God of Creation had spoken to ME. We were not alone. Yes, we had to walk the path of cancer. Yes, there would be some challenges, but we were in His hands. God was walking with us.

God gave us a gift, Living Water for our thirsty souls and a testimony of faithfulness.

John 4

"Now He had to go through Samaria. So He came near a plot of ground Jacob had given to his son Joseph. Jacob's well was there, and Jesus, tired as He was from the journey, sat down by the well. It was about noon. When a Samaritan woman came to draw water, Jesus said to her, 'Will you give me a drink?' (His disciples had gone into town to buy food.) The Samaritan woman said to Him, 'You are a Jew and I am a Samaritan woman. How can You ask me for a drink?' (For Jews do not associate with Samaritans.)" John 4:4-9

Jesus' request was simple, a drink of water.

But...

Jews didn't speak to Samaritans. Not done!

Jewish men did not ask Samaritan women for water. Not ever!

She had made her choices. Her reputation meant that men spoke at her, not to her. She was used to jeering, harassing, suggesting, but it was never water they were after. Her reputation was known in the town, but this was a stranger. This Jew could hardly be aware of her life. Maybe it was because she came alone at the hottest time of the day that gave her away.

But He was only asking for water.

And then He spoke, *"If you knew the gift of God and who it is that asks you for a drink, you would have asked Him and He would have given you living water."* John 4:10

A gift? Living water? For her? Not possible! This stranger did not even have anything with which to draw the water.

"Jesus answered, 'Everyone who drinks this water will be thirsty again, but whoever drinks the water I give them will never thirst. Indeed, the water I give them will become in them a spring of water welling up to eternal life.'

The woman said to him, 'Sir, give me this water so that I won't get thirsty and have to keep coming to draw water.'" John 4:13-15

How lovely it would be to not have to come to this well to get water, to be able to hide out in her little house away from all the comments, and looks. How lovely that would be.

"He told her, 'Go, call your husband and come back.'

'I have no husband', she replied." John 4:16-17

And then Jesus began to tell her that He knew her

past, her present, five husbands and the man she was now living with was not her husband. He knew. He knew her. He knew and yet there were no looks of disgust or disdain, just compassion bubbling over in His eyes. There were no words of condemnation or recriminations, just overwhelming, overpowering love that she wanted to drink in for the rest of her life.

And then she knew. This was more than an offer of freedom from the well; this was freedom from her past.

Living water was more than a drink. It was the well itself, and the offer was to her.

And the offer still stands.

Day 8

We prayed for healing. I do believe that God could have simply touched John and healed him. For some unseen reason, surgery was the route we needed to go. We would trust that God had a plan.

We waited as John went into the operating room. The waiting room is a difficult place to be, both in the hospital and in life. Finally the surgeon came to talk to us. The surgery went well. John did well. But the surgeon could not tell if the cancer had spread. He did not know at that time if we would need further treatments or more aggressive action. We would need to wait until the testing of all the tissue came back. Wait... wait. The waiting room is hard when you want answers now.

The next morning I went to the Lord with a question. *"Why?"* This was not *"Why us?"*, or *"Why John?"*, although if those are our questions I believe God is big enough to handle them. This was the why of *"Why are we here?"* I picked up my Bible and turned to Luke 5.

Jesus was by the lake. He was teaching and Jesus said to Simon Peter in verse 4. *"Put out into the deep water and let down the nets for a catch."*

As I read I remember saying to the Lord, *"That's how I feel, like we are in the deep water."*

I do not like deep water. I start to hyperventilate just thinking about it. I had to be pulled out of a lake once as a little girl and it left me with a great fear of the deep water. I'm good if I can touch the bottom. I'm okay if I don't have my head under, but the deep water is not where I want to be.

But the deep water was where we were.

"Simon answered, 'Master we've worked hard all night and haven't caught anything. But because You say so, I will let down the nets.' When they had done so, they caught such a large number of fish that their nets began to break." Luke 5:4-6

A familiar passage but a stunning new message for me because God spoke, *"Do you see? The deep water is where the fish are."*

What? Wow! The fish are in the deep water. We were in the deep water. We as believers are called to be fishers of men, and the deep water is where the fish are. Wait, this cancer was not just random, there was purpose here, purpose in the cancer, purpose in the hospital, purpose for John and me. We were there not just to get well, but to be on mission, an assignment from God Himself.

As John recuperated, they changed his room so many times I lost count, different roommates, different families, different moments to minister. Prayer, sharing the good news, a book for a nurse who told me she was getting married. Her words, *"I want a marriage like yours."*

That was an open door, I was delighted to share. I simply told her, it was not just about the two of us, our marriage was about a relationship with Jesus.

Mission. God had told me to be on the lookout for the fish there in the deep water.

By the way the cancer for John was over when we left the hospital. We got to close that chapter. It doesn't mean that we might not have to reopen that book someday, but God's faithfulness made it a miracle memory.

Luke 5, Matthew 4

In first century Israel, every child went to school to learn Torah, the first five books of the Bible, but then for most, school was over. The girls worked at home learning to become Godly wives and mothers. The boys went on to become apprentices in their fathers' businesses. However, a few, the best, were picked to learn more. Those young men studied, they memorized all of the Scripture until, out of that select few, a handful qualified to become a disciple to a rabbi. Only the sharpest, the most brilliant, most astute were chosen. The remainder went home to work with Dad. So becoming a disciple to a Rabbi was a coveted position, and only a few achieved it. The best of the best were picked to become disciples.

Peter and Andrew had been out fishing. James and John were in a boat, fishing with their father. These boys were fishermen. What does that tell us? They weren't already disciples to a famous rabbi. They had not made the cut. They were not the best of the best. They weren't the brightest, the sharpest, the over achievers. They were working in the family business, fishing. They were the ordinary kids, not the kids who got picked for the excel program.

But Jesus walked by. Matthew 4:19. *"Come, follow me," Jesus said, "and I will send you out to fish for people."* The King James Version says it like this,

"Follow me and I will make you fishers of men."

Jesus, the most famous Rabbi of all time, was calling to them. Jesus, the One who could have chosen the brightest, the best, the most qualified, was choosing them. Jesus wanted just ordinary people to become His disciples.

It wasn't about how able, or smart or qualified Peter, Andrew, James and John were. It was absolutely about how able He is. It was not about their brilliance. It was about the brilliance of the Son of God.

They did not have to be the best, the most, the finest.

The qualification is not that we must be; the promise is that He will make us to become...because HE IS.

Day 9

I have a question for you. It is a powerful question and a thought-provoking question. So here it is...

How would you like to be remembered?

Take a few moments to think that over and then write it in one sentence.

All right. This is how you would like to be remembered. But do you think that's what people would actually say?

Maybe not? Then write the reality. There it is. Your life summed up in one sentence. Pick it up and take a good look.

Any changes? Content with what you have there in your hand?

Now let's say that those words are the ones that will echo through eternity about you. As the door closes here and opens there, are you really okay with that?

So let me pose a few other questions. They are even more thought provoking and even more powerful. So here they are...

Is that what God wants your life to say?
Has your life counted for more than just what you think is important?
Has your life counted for the eternal?
Is it worth every breath you have taken?
Is this the message that you would want to echo through the heavens?
Did you use what you have?
Are you making money or making a difference?
Are you building your kingdom or building The Kingdom?
You aren't taking any of it with you, so was it worth it?

How do we answer this? How do we shake out our daily lives to point to the eternal? How do we sift through what seems mundane to make it count?

I have a statement for you. It is a powerful statement and a thought provoking statement. Here it is...

Live with the end in mind!

Matthew 14

John the Baptist...we've talked about him before. There wasn't much applause where he lived. He was okay with that. He was a man behind the scenes but before the people.

But even that was taken from him.

"Now Herod had arrested John and bound him and put him in prison because of Herodias, his brother Philip's wife, John had been saying to him: 'It is not lawful for you to have her.'" Matthew 14:3-4

He had lived his life in the fresh air. His life ended in the stench of a first century pit.

The sweetness of honey had been a big part of his diet. His prison food was probably thrown through the bars onto the filth underfoot. His voice had thundered as he baptized. Could it even be heard over the curses and screams that came out of the prison walls?

He had been bound to his mission in the wilderness. Was he bound by chains in the cell?

The crowds began to understand freedom, as he proclaimed truth and repentance to all who would hear. His freedom was taken from him because he proclaimed truth and repentance to those who refused to hear. But stench and filth and cells would not, could not, quiet a life that was lived with the end in mind.

He took his last breath under the blade of a sword. His head was placed on a platter and brought to King Herod. Herod's family thought that John's death would quiet his voice of truth. But death cannot quiet truth. His voice still echoes.

John lived his life with the end in mind because he knew that the end was only the beginning!

Day 10

My out of town children and grandchildren came home for a visit. They stayed at my house, but unfortunately I had to leave town for some of that time. Grandma's house is fun because grandmothers don't always think that a little extra sugar is necessarily a bad thing. And it's also kind of fun because there are fewer rules. But even at Grandma's house there have to be some, like: don't play with knives, don't run next to the open staircase and don't lock your brothers and sisters in the bedrooms. But we never thought we needed a rule that pointy objects should not be plunged into blown-up balloon-like balls. Maybe we should have gotten to that one.

I got a call while I was gone.

The little voice at the other end of the phone said, *"I'm sorry."* Then there were garbled, incoherent words that I couldn't decipher. He was crying. My daughter had handed him the phone when I answered and my grandson was trying to tell me he had broken something. I couldn't understand him so I asked again to speak to his mom.

Katie explained. He had decided to experiment with a decorative pick pulled out of a flower arrangement and the exercise ball that I kept in the basement. He wanted to see what would happen when the two met.

A pretty entertaining thing happened. That very sharp pick went directly into the ball. But then shortly after that, the exercise ball began changing a little at a time. Before his eyes it was turning from a large round exercise ball into a shriveled, deflated exercise mat. Yes, it was flattened. Suddenly he realized maybe that wasn't such a good experiment.

It was pretty obvious to his parents that it wasn't a good choice.

Since the ball is designed to hold an adult's entire weight, patching was not an option. The only thing to do was throw it away. My daughter wanted him to tell me that. She handed him back the phone. *"Tell her what happened."*

And he tried. His little quacking, quivering voice finally choked out, *"Will you forgive me?"*

Would I forgive him? Absolutely. There is not one thing on this planet that my grandchildren could do that would make me not forgive them. I love them so much, so passionately, so unconditionally and I always will.

I assured him that it was okay. I forgave him but then I asked to speak again to his mom. *"Katie, it's really okay, you see the..."*

She interrupted, *"No, Mom it isn't okay. We will replace it."*

"No, it really is okay as far as I'm concerned. The exercise ball isn't mine. It belongs to your sister, Julie."

My poor grandson had to go through this again.

We are sinners. We do wrong stuff every day. My little grandson was caught in his sin. I am grateful that my children are teaching my grandchildren to own up to their sins and ask for forgiveness. It is what we want them to do with Jesus.

We must come to Him and own up to our sin. He is the one we have sinned against and we must ask Him for forgiveness.

And you know what? He will always forgive. There is not one thing on the planet that we can do that He will not forgive. He loves us so much, so passionately, so unconditionally and He always will.

John 8

She was made to stand in their midst. She had been caught. How had it happened?

Was it a set-up? Was the design of this to not only catch her and therefore rid their world of one more harlot, or was it also to catch Jesus, to put Him into a no-win situation? The Bible tells us in John 8 that they wanted to trap Jesus, so the teachers of the law and the Pharisees had brought her, standing her before the crowd. Here she was, this spectacle of ridicule and a soon to be recipient of the death sentence, that they were sure would follow.

Stoning...picking up large rocks and aiming them at her, throwing them at vital body parts to make the kill shot, or possibly lobbing them at extremities to make the execution and therefore the lesson drag on even longer. Today would be a good day for a lesson.

So, as the crowd gathered, she stood, waiting, most likely knowing she was at death's door. The leaders spoke. *"Teacher, this woman was caught in the act of adultery. In the Law Moses commanded us to stone such women. Now what do you say?"*
John 8:4-5

So what did Jesus say?

He said nothing. He bent down and began to write with His finger in the dirt. What did He write? We don't know. The Bible doesn't tell us. What we do know is that it was the finger of God that had etched the words of the Law into the stone tablets on Mt. Sinai. Now here was God incarnate writing with His finger in the dirt.

Whatever He wrote was powerful because as they continued to question, He straightened up and then said to them, *"Let any of you who is without sin be the first to throw a stone at her."* John 8:7

Jesus bent down and once again began to write. Little by little, from the older ones first, they began to walk away. Soon they were gone. Jesus once again straightened and this time questioned her. *"Woman, where are they? Has no one condemned you?"*

"No one, sir." she said.

No words of rebuke or condemnation, Jesus said, *"Then neither do I condemn you...Go now and leave your life of sin."* John 8:10-11

From condemnation to forgiveness, from death to life...

Was it a good day for a lesson? Yes, it sure was. The lesson was this: There is no sin too big for Jesus to forgive. We can come condemned and leave forgiven when we come to Jesus. We can be standing at death's door and with His words of forgiveness, we can leave having eternal life.

Day 11

I love purses. I'm not exactly sure why, but I love them. Maybe it's because they always fit. It doesn't matter if I lose fifteen pounds and gain back five, the purse still fits. (Now if you are a man reading this, hang on, it will be okay.) My husband indulges me at Christmas and my birthday and sometimes for no reason at all. He knows I really like purses. He allows me to buy a new purse now and then. It's not that I need them, but they're fun. Besides, there is a little verse in the Bible that I have grown to love. It is in Luke 12:33 *"Provide purses for yourself that will not wear out..."* My brother Bill says that most likely the original Greek may have said something like... provide "power tools" for yourself that will not wear out. (Yes, I know...not correct exegesis.)

One night I was watching a purse show and I must have been exhausted. I just don't fall asleep during purse shows. (Again, if you're a man, aren't you glad you're hanging in here with me cause now you've learned that there are PURSE SHOWS!)

My husband came to bed and the show was still on. He started watching it. Understand my husband is a man's man. He played football in high school, college and would have played pro football had he not sustained a major injury. He's the guy that would break a finger and just say *"Ahhhh, tape it up. I'm going back in."* He became a world-class weight lifter. But, here was this man's man watching a purse show. Why? Because he loves me. He told me the next day the colors and styles he liked. How about that for sweet!

You see he lays aside his wants, his desires, his life, for me...like Jesus did for us.

Several months ago we experienced a terribly turbulent storm in our lives. Our dear Mother had to have surgery and then some very painful, traumatic procedures, more surgery, which brought more extreme pain, and eventually she died. I say it was a storm because I felt like I was caught in the swirling, heart stopping wind of a violent tornado. About the time we thought it was calming even a little, it would pick back up and get more violent. Then days of events followed that were exhausting and sad. Please understand, I do not grieve one moment for her, because I know where she is and she stands in the presence of Jesus. But simply stated I miss her.

During this time my husband wanted to bless me, so he bought me a purse. He could have used that money to buy himself a power tool. But he wanted to bless me. Did it erase the storm? No, but it was a little reminder that he was riding out this storm with me.

Luke 8

I cannot imagine being in a violent storm in a boat on a lake.

Yet, that is where Jesus was with His disciples. He had said to them, *"Let us go over to the other side of the lake."* Luke 8:22

So they climbed into the boat to head across. As they sailed, Jesus fell asleep. Sometimes we look at Jesus and forget that although He was fully God, He was also fully human. Yes, He was a man's man and He was God-man, but He got tired. He experienced exhaustion. Healing those who were sick, casting out evil spirits, dealing with clamoring crowds, teaching...Jesus got tired. His body needed rest, just like ours do.

And then...

"A squall came down on the lake, so that the boat was being swamped, and they were in great danger." Luke 8:23

This word in the Greek actually means hurricane kind of winds. This caused the boat to be swamped, overtaken by water. It was violent and this boat, with Jesus and the disciples in it, was in great danger.

And Jesus was asleep. Asleep in the middle of a

storm, it is such a picture of perfect peace. But the disciples were not experiencing peace. They were frantic and woke Him. *"Master, Master, we're going to drown."* Luke 8:24a

So did this catch Jesus by surprise? Did he shake Himself from the sleepiness and proceed to worry?

"He got up and rebuked the wind and the raging waters; the storm subsided and all was calm. 'Where is your faith?' He asked his disciples." Luke 8:24b-25

A storm on a lake, no matter how violent, doesn't catch Jesus by surprise. The storms in our lives, no matter how violent, don't catch Jesus by surprise. He can rebuke the wind or He can help us navigate through it. This is the question that Jesus also asks us, *"Where is your faith?"* Because, either way, He can bring peace in the midst of a storm, just ask Him.

Day 12

Celebration Day

Psalm 145

"I will exalt you my God the King..."

As you read Psalm 145 today, magnify His name.

Day 13

What breaks in your heart and your head when you look at someone else and think you can overpower them? He was fifteen, but looked at the woman and knew he could. He did. So much so that it stole her life from her.

He was fifteen. Now he was a rapist and murderer. He was dangerous and terrible.

Did the police catch him right away? No.

Did the detectives working the case put the clues together and figure out he had done it? No.

Can a person get away with a crime like that?

Let me say this. Whether a criminal is caught or not, the answer to that question is *"No. A person cannot get away with a crime like that."*

Because God knew and because he knew.

He knew that he had been the one who had taken her life. Every morning as he rose and looked at himself in the mirror, he knew. Every night, when he tried to rest his head on his pillow, to attempt yet another fitful night's sleep, he knew. Every day as he tried to fill up the day with enough noise to drown out the sound of her fear, he knew.

Had he gotten away with it? Absolutely not!

The guilt, the pain, the horror of what he had done, drove him to one day walk into the police station and turn himself in.

It was not a life for a life. She had died; he received a prison sentence. Turning himself in did not take away the guilt. He was paying for the crime. He was in prison, but it did not soothe the pain in his heart.

But in the prison cell he found something. It was a Gideon Bible. He began to read it. There was also a woman who came to visit him. She kept telling him he could be forgiven. Her voice echoed the words he was reading.

Could it be possible that he, who had been so wicked, could actually be forgiven?

Could it be possible that this One he was reading about could reach down and forgive him?

Could the Savior have come and died for him?

Wasn't he too wicked to be saved?

Little by the little the truth of the Word reached into

his heart and he believed. Jesus, the One who came to die for wicked sinners, had come for even him.

He was not too wicked to be saved, and this man asked Jesus to be his Savior.

Today he shares that same message with others.

Luke 8

Too wicked to be saved?

Maybe we've thought that about someone. Maybe we've thought that about ourselves. Too wicked to be saved...is that possible?

Jesus had calmed the storm, so they finished the trip. They went to the region of the Gerasenes across the lake from Galilee. Jesus stepped out of the boat and met a man, a wild man. This man was broken both in his heart and in his head. He was demon possessed. He cut himself. He didn't wear clothes. He did not live in a house. He was a dead man walking. He lived among the tombs. He was so feared that others attempted to restrain him by binding him hand and foot and keeping him under guard. It made no difference; he couldn't be restrained and he would break the chains and go off.

But now he was here, crying out at the feet of Jesus, who had crossed the lake.

Jesus always knows exactly how to get to the heart of someone and He confronted the evil.

Luke 8:30-31 *"Jesus asked him, 'What is your name?' 'Legion,' he replied, because many demons had gone into him. And they begged Jesus repeatedly not to order them to go into the Abyss."*

I'm going to pause for just a moment and ask you to reflect. If the demons are terrified to go to the bottomless pit, if they don't want to go to the Abyss to be tortured, how much more should we be afraid not only for ourselves, but also for our loved ones and friends?

The demons begged Jesus to send them anywhere but to the Abyss. Jesus did an amazing thing by calling this legion of demons out of the man and they headed into a lake packed in pork.

Later the people came to see what had happened. The pigs were gone. The demons were gone. And the man? The man was dressed, in his right mind, and sitting next to the Savior.

He begged Jesus to allow him to go with Him but Jesus sent him back, saying, *"Return home and tell how much God has done for you."* Luke 8:39

The man went back home and did exactly that, telling others what God had done. He had encountered the Savior and his life for eternity was changed. What a story!

So did you see what happened here? This man was wicked. He was dangerous and terrible and could not be controlled. That is until Jesus made it a point to go across the lake, even in a storm, to meet one man...this man, the demon possessed man of the Gerasenes. The one who many might have said was too wicked to be saved.

Jesus went for one.

Day 14

I am going to be transparent. I am going to be graphic. I am not the woman with the issue of blood, but I have been. I did not have to say *"unclean"* everywhere I went, but I felt unclean.

Twenty years ago I needed surgery, but until that happened, I was dealing with this issue. After a night of hemorrhaging, I would somehow pull myself out of bed, pale and weak, to get ready for work.

Now I am going to be embarrassingly transparent because I know other people have gone through this too. I had left the world of diapers years before, but because of this issue, almost every day I had to put on an adult diaper which had a plastic coating that crinkled. At that time it was my only workable option. Today there are movie stars that advertise silent, slim, unnoticeable options even under close fitting red carpet attire. These come in designer colors, and can be worn while dancing with stars and not a single person will know. (Why didn't I take this idea to the Sharks?) But, you see, twenty years ago thick, crackling diapers were the only choice. So I would stuff myself into tight black tights (thus the word tights) when I wore my black skirt or navy blue tights with my dark blue one. I did this to stifle the telltale noise from the diaper.

One day black, one day blue, the next day black, and then again blue, those two outfits were my alternatives.

I once had a student jokingly tell me I was a sharp dresser. I wanted to jokingly fail him in the course.

Now I am going to be even more embarrassingly transparent. One day I had to leave work because all of a sudden I started hemorrhaging and I had left my diapers at home. It was terrible and by the time I got home I was a mess. There was a trail of blood from the car to the house.

Now...go back 2,000 years. No diapers, no tights, no keeping it quiet, spending everything she had on doctors and no results.

Luke 8

His heart was breaking. He was in such pain. He had known the joy of fatherhood for TWELVE short years. He adored his child. But today his little girl was close to death, with every breath her life was ebbing away.

Jairus was a ruler in the synagogue, a leader. That lofty position gave him standing in the community. It afforded him respect. But position, respect could not heal his little girl. He could not save his child's life.

So Jairus went to find the One who could help. He went to Jesus.

And when he found Him, Jairus threw pride and position to the wind, fell on his face and begged. He pleaded with Jesus to come to his house.

And you know what? Jesus went with him. Jesus came to Jairus' side and began walking with him to his home.

But then...

Her heart was breaking. She was in such pain. She had known the shame of uncleanness for TWELVE long years. She was sick, constantly bleeding, with every beat of her heart, her life was ebbing away. It made her impure, unclean, untouchable. Her lowly position meant she lived away, apart.

But suddenly a miracle, Jesus was passing by and Jesus could heal.

She threw her shame and caution to the wind and reached for what was impossible. She should not touch, and yet she dared. She knew that her impurity would affect His purity and still she reached for the fringe of His prayer shawl. With her touch she begged. With the slightest brush of her fingers she pleaded for healing.

The Scripture in Malachi 4:2 says, *"But unto you that fear my name shall the Son of Righteousness arise with healing in His wings..."* Such a beautiful promise that the Messiah would heal. (By the way the sides of the prayer shawl are called the wings. I just love that and wanted to share.)

And then...instantly she knew...His touch had extended to her. His healing was all over her.

Then came the question.

"Who touched me?"

Peter answered, *"Master, the people are crowding and pressing against you."* Luke 8:45

Jesus knew. He already knew who it was, but His

love for this child of His would not allow her to live the rest of her life believing she had stolen the healing, rather than it being given. Jesus wanted her to own it.

"Someone has touched me; I know that power has gone out from me."

"Then the woman, seeing that she could not go unnoticed, came trembling and fell at His feet. In the presence of all the people, she told why she had touched Him and how she had been instantly healed. Then He said to her, 'Daughter, your faith has healed you. Go in peace.'" Luke 8:46-48

"Daughter!"

Did you hear that, He called HER *"daughter"*? This obscure, unclean, unnamed woman, Jesus called her daughter. It is the only time in the Scripture when Jesus calls someone daughter. She was His child. She was as much His daughter as Jairus' little girl was his. Jesus cared about this outcast woman every bit as much as Jairus cared for his child. Jesus wanted His child healed as much as Jairus did.

And indeed she was healed. Twelve long, lonely years were healed in a nanosecond.

But even a nanosecond was precious time, time that Jairus' little girl did not have. And by the time this miracle was over, Jairus' little girl's time had run out.

Verse 49, *"While Jesus was still speaking, someone came from the house of Jairus, the synagogue leader. 'Your daughter is dead,' he said. 'Don't bother the teacher anymore.'"*

"Don't bother the teacher anymore."

Horrible, awful words, He was too late. Jesus was too late.

Too late, too late, Jairus' precious little girl was dead. Jesus had stopped to help someone else and now it was too late for his child.

Can you imagine the grief? Can you feel his pain? If Jesus had not stopped, Jairus' daughter might have lived. But now it was too late. His beautiful little girl was dead. The small window of opportunity was closed. The door was locked and the key thrown away. All hope was gone.

Why bother the teacher anymore?

And then Jesus' lovely words in verse 50, *"Hearing this, Jesus said to Jairus, 'Don't be afraid; just believe, and she will be healed.'"*

Hope for the hopeless, these are beautiful words.

"Don't be afraid, just believe."

"Why bother the Teacher?"

Why bother? Because He doesn't just have the answer, He is the Answer. Jesus took the little girl by the hand and spoke. Instantly her spirit returned.

Day 15

There are some things that you experience that make you want to jump out of the tub into a pot of boiling water. And so it was on this particular day.

Oh, and just so you know, this story happened at my house. I have a whirlpool tub.

I know, I just made you envious.

Don't be.

First rule: Don't get a whirlpool tub unless you know what you are doing.

Second rule: Get the stuff that will clean out the jets.

Who knew?

It had been a great evening Bible study. We could see on faces that some of those *"Ah ha"* moments were going on. Those are the times when you get to see things in the Scripture that you never knew before. It was a fun night, a real mountain top experience. But you do then have to come down off the mountain.

Next morning I was reflecting as I was having Bible study. It felt like one of those days that you just want to get a little more coffee, stay in your chair and study a little more. But daily life is daily life and I needed to get moving.

So jump in the tub, get the jets going, get the steam rising and get ready to face the day. I did. I don't wear glasses in the tub so the world of soapsuds and washcloths is a little blurry, but that usually doesn't matter. I did notice that the tub seemed to have some flecks of dirt and wondered what the last person to use the tub had scrubbed off. Wait! That was me. It was probably just a little lint from the dark washcloth I was using.

I grabbed my glasses to check.

Whirlpool jets make the water move. It feels a little like living water. And so it was on this day. But as I turned off the jets, the foam settled.

But the little flecks of lint didn't. And there weren't just a few. The bubbles had masked the reality.

Suddenly I recognized the problem. These were black worms. How big were they? I really don't know. They have maybe grown with the re-telling.

Black, wiggling, disgusting...What were those?

Honestly, I didn't care if I found out the kingdom, genus, phylum, warm or cold-blooded. The only classification I cared about was living and nonliving.

You can't even begin to grasp the speed with which you can exit a worm-filled tub. Why hadn't I asked Santa Claus for lye soap that could be rubbed directly onto my skin as I tried to scrape off any of the writhing slugs? Lye soap is made from ashes and can clean up just about anything. I think it is one of the perks to sackcloth and ashes.

Who knew?

But without the lye, I did the best I could. I didn't care what I grabbed to put on. I didn't care about my make-up, hair, or nails.

Some things move to the back of the line when you are worm hunting. Haven't you found that to be true? And some things move to the front of the line.

Finding ammunition was one of those.

I didn't care what this was going to take. Drain cleaner, toilet bowl scrub, rat poison, or a combination of toxic chemicals that made my house smell like we needed a meth bust. The tub could have exploded for all I cared.

The phone rang. I didn't want to take the call. I was headed out to buy a HAZMAT suit.

But my husband answered. It was his brother. He started the conversation with, *"Now, no one is hurt...but...Charity just had an accident right here by my house. She saw me, waved and rear-ended the car in front of her."*

Boy, was I ever glad we had taught her to be so polite. Somehow I think she missed the lesson on looking where you are driving.

Suddenly de-worming a tub took on a little different urgency.

We ran to the car.

Everybody really was okay and the cars weren't that broken.

I was even able to buy an assortment of poisons that day. It is always good to have poison on hand for the day worms come over. That way you have something for them to eat.

I haven't used the whirlpool jets since.

By the way, just forget about this little conversation if you ever see a *"For Sale"* sign in my yard. I really don't know the rules when it comes to full disclosure on property...but I promise I will find out.

Matthew 17

Today, let's walk with Jesus up the Mount of Transfiguration along with Peter, James, and John. If we're followers then we belong there too. Jesus is taking us to pray. His ministry is bathed in prayer.

The challenge today is unspoken, but certainly we feel it. If He needed to pray, then how much more do we? But as often happens in prayer, sleepiness seems to intervene. The warmth of the sun, the exhaustion from the climb, it's hard not to give into it.

But then suddenly, everything is changed. Jesus face is shining like the sun. His clothes are a brilliant white, like a flash of lighting. Now fully awake, we see His glory. For a brief moment the veil has been pulled back and we are given a glimpse of His Heavenly Presence, His beauty, His radiance, His splendor. There aren't words big enough to describe it.

Moses and Elijah are with Him, somehow we recognize them. They're clothed in that same radiant light, talking with Jesus, just talking, such an ordinary thing, for such an extraordinary moment. Is this a glimpse of what we will someday experience? The familiar mixed with exquisite beauty, being clothed in His brilliant light, able to just talk with our Beloved, knowing each person. God has given us such a gift, a taste, a hint of what awaits us someday in Heaven.

But then it is time to come down off the mountain. We can't just live on the mountaintop.

And so it was with the disciples, Peter, James and John came down off the mountain. Suddenly they were faced with a situation that they couldn't solve. The mountain had been wonderful, but daily life crowded in. Unexpected situations interrupted the bliss.

Fear, helplessness, terror gripped the father.
Convulsions, screaming, a demon gripped the son.
This father stood by helplessly.
He watched as his child was being destroyed.
The medical world didn't have the answer.
The teachers of the law didn't have the answer.
Even the disciples couldn't help.

But this helplessness brought the father to the only One who could help. His desperation made him desperate to see Jesus. This incredible, overwhelming, heart-wrenching circumstance was the very thing that brought both father and son to meet Christ.

The father pleaded with Jesus in Matthew 17:15-16, *"'Lord, have mercy on my son,' he said. 'He has seizures and is suffering greatly. He often falls into the fire or into the water. I brought him to your disciples, but they could not heal him.'"*

A few words, a simple prayer, and that was enough, because remember, Jesus didn't just have the answer...He was the Answer. And the boy was healed.

Day 16

My sister-in-law is sweet, kind and giving. I have always looked forward to having her and my brother-in-law come into town. We have laughed and cried together, but more often than not, we have laughed. For some reason the two of us seem to wander into funny stories.

She told me a story about her boys when they were little. There was a man in their neighborhood that she didn't necessarily want her kids to be around. He was a stranger. Although she didn't invent the idea of stranger danger, it just came naturally to be overprotective. It wasn't that he was a bad man, she just didn't know enough about him.

Parents want to protect. We want to shelter our children from every harsh or terrible thing in the world. It's impossible, but we try and sometimes in our efforts we make quick judgments, rash decisions that are based on instinct or feelings rather than reality.

She didn't go into great detail with her children. She didn't explain why. She merely told the two boys to stay away from him.

But somehow her older son came to his own conclusions as to why his mother did not want him to be around this man.

One day there was a knock at the door. It was a warm day and the only door locked was a screen door. Her son went to the door as children sometimes do. He could have said, *"Just a minute please, I'll go get my mom."* He could have done several things that would have made the outcome different. But what he did was to stand at the door and yell at the top of his lungs. *"Ma-um, it's the yucky, dirty man that you ha-ate!"*

Can you hear it? The almost song like sentence wafting high into the air over only one audience member, the very man he was yelling about.

She had never said *'yucky'* about this man.

She had not used the word *'dirty'*.

'Hate' had never been connected with this man's name. But somehow her son had linked all of those words with not only his name, but his face and his whole being.

How do you recover from that? How do you paint that into a follow-up sentence that buys it back?

My sister-in-law was mortified. She had to face the man. He was standing at her door.

Sometimes being a good parent makes you feel like not such a good neighbor.

Luke 10

"On one occasion an expert in the law stood up to test Jesus. 'Teacher,' he asked, 'what must I do to inherit eternal life?'

'What is written in the law?' He replied. 'How do you read it?'

He answered, 'Love the Lord your God with all your heart and with all your soul and with all your strength and with all your mind, and, love your neighbor as yourself.'

'You have answered correctly,' Jesus replied. 'Do this and you will live.'

But he wanted to justify himself, so he asked Jesus, 'And who is my neighbor?'" Luke 10:25-29

The first question was to test Jesus. The second was to justify himself.

In reply Jesus began to tell a story:

A man was traveling from Jerusalem to Jericho when he fell into the hands of robbers. He was stripped, beaten and left half dead.

A priest happened to be going down that same road. He saw the man, but passed by on the other side. A

Levite did the same. But a Samaritan came to where the nearly dead man was and when he saw him, he took pity on the injured man. The Samaritan poured oil on the wounds, bandaged them, put the man on his own donkey, took him to an inn, took care of him, paid for his care, left, but promised to return and pay any and all additional debt.

In verse 37 Jesus asked, *"Which of these three do you think was a neighbor to the man who fell into the hands of robbers?*

The expert in the law replied, 'The one who had mercy on him.'

Jesus told him, 'Go and do likewise.'"

We can see that Jesus so beautifully answered the question that the expert in the law posed about who is my neighbor. But did Jesus simply ignore the question about what someone must do to inherit eternal life?

Let's look at that story again.

All of us are like the man in the story. Satan has robbed us, stolen from us. John 10:10 tells us, *"The thief comes only to steal and kill and destroy; I have come that they may have life and have it to the full."*

Since the Garden of Eden, satan has robbed mankind. We have been stripped and left dying in our sins. We need someone to help us.

But like the priest in the story, religion cannot save us. The Law, like the Levite, condemns us.

We need someone like the Samaritan to rescue us. The Samaritans were hated because they were half-breeds. Jews and Assyrians married and had children. So the Samaritans were a picture of someone from two different worlds and the Jews rejected them, hated them, scorned them. Jesus fully God and fully man came, but He was rejected, hated and scorned. And like the Samaritan, He came to where mankind was. He came to us in our sinful, broken, wounded state. He came to bind up our wounds, pay all of our debt and care for all our needs.

Once done, He left with a promise to return. And did you see in the story what else He promised to do? While He was gone, if there was any more debt, any more cost, any more payment, that would be paid for too.

What must we do to inherit eternal life? Recognize that we cannot save ourselves and say *"Yes"* to the One who can.

Day 17

There are some things that you experience that make you want to jump into a tub filled with scouring powder. And so it was in this particular class. Oh, and just so you know, the teacher was a sub, in a middle school class, with a group of students she had never met. Ever been a sub, in a middle school class, with a group of students you have never met?

First Rule: Maintain order.

Second Rule: Realize that everything that students tell you may not always be exactly the truth.

Third Rule: Believe them when they tell you they are going to throw up.

Fourth Rule: If a middle school student asks to exit the room, have him leave one of his shoes so you know he will come back.

Substitute Teacher: "Students, when I call your name please raise your hand and say *'Here.'*"

Student: (interrupting) *"Something back here smells really bad."*

(Sidebar: In a middle school classroom, bad smells

kind of go with the territory. The regular teacher kept a can of air freshener on her desk.)

Substitute Teacher: (still attempting to maintain order... in a firm voice) *"Thanks for telling me."* (continues with roll call)

Student: (interrupting, gagging vehemently) *"I'm not kidding, something back here smells REALLY BAD. I think I'm going to be sick."*

Different Student: (walking up to the front of the classroom, whispering) *"Could I please go to the restroom to wash off my shoes? I think I must have stepped where my dog was this morning."*

Fifth Rule: Feel free to break rule number four if a student has stepped where his dog was.

TIME: 8:15 AM. Subs DO NOT get paid enough!

Luke 11

"Mommy, will you...?" 'Daddy, can you...?" "Mom, would you...?" "Dad, I need..." "Teacher, there is..."

"Mommy... Daddy...Mom...Dad...Teacher?" Children know how to ask, ask again, keep on asking and asking and asking and asking. If we are parents, grandparents, teachers... you get the idea, we've lived that kind of request from our children. They are bold and diligent in their ability to ask for their needs to be met.

In Luke 11 Jesus said that is how bold we can be with our requests to our Heavenly Father. When we're hurting, troubled or afraid, when we have a need or a burden we're carrying, when something seems so big or impossible or even too little to be bothered with, we can bring those needs to the Lord.

And then, when in the next few minutes that wave of hurt or panic or sadness or fear comes again, we can ask again and again and again. God doesn't tell us to stop or get upset with our requests. Instead He so lovingly wraps His arms around us and gives rest.

Luke 11 sums it up...ask, keep on asking, seek, keep on seeking, knock and keep on knocking. If we know how to lovingly answer our children's requests, how much more will God Almighty so lovingly answer ours?

So how do we pray?

Luke 11:1 *"One day Jesus was praying in a certain place. When He finished, one of the disciples said to Him, 'Lord, teach us to pray, just as John taught his disciples to pray.'"*

So when this disciple asked Jesus to teach them to pray, he did it because Jesus prayed. Jesus prayed in solitude, sometimes in a crowd, at times with a few. He prayed standing, kneeling, walking. Jesus prayed all night, but sometimes His prayers were very short. He praised God, thanked God, worshiped God, blessed the Name of God. He prayed for healing. He interceded, sometimes weeping, sometimes with great joy. He prayed fervently. He prayed conversationally. Jesus lived prayer, breathed prayer, modeled prayer, and taught prayer. In other words, Jesus prayed.

Seems a little daunting doesn't it? But this is where you begin, *"Father."*

Day 18

Two of our children were in the hospital, one for some minor surgery, another for tests because of the possibility of a brain tumor. So from surgery to brain scans, it was a pretty exhausting couple of days. The girls were little, three and five, so they couldn't grasp the fact that they weren't allowed to eat the night before all the medical stuff. They were hungry and cranky and crying. I kept thinking, *"When will this day end?"* But little did I know, the end was nowhere in sight. The surgery went well. The tests proved negative. Thankfully, it was time to head home to rest.

And then, another bomb shell.

"Oh and yes, one of the children does have pin worms."

"No!"

"Yes!"

Previously we wrote about an aversion to worms, creeping, crawling, wiggling around outside in the wide-open spaces or hiding in whirlpool jets. But they can actually pretty much be avoided on a daily basis, until you're told that they have moved in and are now dwelling in one's personal space. These puppies live in the large intestine. They dine on the stuff we don't want on our shoes. HATE doesn't describe the feeling.

Getting rid of them becomes PRIORITY ONE.

Never had this experience? OHHHH, let me be the one to tell you how it works. I'm an expert.

First, everyone in the entire family gets to enjoy the deliciousness of anti-worm medicine. Everyone! You see pin worms like to explore, so everyone in the house is at risk. The birthday money you were saving needs to go somewhere, why not on something that kills. You swallow with the hope that those wriggling crawling things soon meet a screaming, burning death. Too harsh? Ummm, let me think about that? No screaming, burning, pretty much sums it up. And then you wait for the funeral of those vile creatures. It is the same fate as a dead gold fish and with a flush they are out of your life for good.

Sounds simple enough doesn't it? But you see it isn't that simple because the de-worm-ification process has only just begun. (I'm hearing the lyrics to an old Karen Carpenter's song.) Yes, the medicine is swallowed, followed by those critters soon being deposited dead, dead as a doornail on the other side with a message written inside the colon of the entire family. NO VACANCY!

But until the death occurs there can be babies crawling in the bathrooms or on the sheets, or in the clothes, tiny minuscule worms or worm eggs, or maybe even worm moms or dads or brothers or sisters, or aunts or uncles, huddled masses yearning to breathe free, who escape their confines for a brief moment of fresh air. If your home was a colon wouldn't you want a bit of fresh air? These are survivor types who lie in wait for the medicine to lose its punch and then revisit.

SOOOO the whole house has to be cleaned. All the sheets washed, every single day for at least a week. All the clothes, all the time, from morning till night, I've been working in the laundry room all the livelong day. The bathrooms need to be cleaned every time, EVERY SINGLE TIME someone uses them. Good, good times! The children's toys need to be cleaned or bagged up or stored because little hands do not always get washed sparkling clean and there could be a not yet dead worm waiting to pounce. The floor around the beds must be vacuumed time and time again. This is all followed up with one more round of medicine and there goes the Easter outfit money. In the end, the house is sparkling clean, the colon a whole lot cleaner, and the bank account cleaned out.

The only thing that's as much fun is when you have

to buy HEAD LICE MEDICINE! Never had this experience? Again, I'm an expert. Makes you want to visit me.

So here's the point, some things are better learned by reading than by doing. I'm just saying.

De-worm-ification, anti-lice stuff, we really can get enough info to last us the rest of our lives just by reading about it.

But then, there are those things we need to actually do in order to learn. Learning to drive, we can read about it, study it, but until we actually get behind the wheel we won't be drivers.

Cooking, we can read about it, study recipes, but until we actually walk into the kitchen, we won't become cooks. And prayer, we can read about it. We can study what others have written about it. But to really learn to pray, we must pray. To experience the power of prayer, we can't just read about it, we must be the ones to pray.

Luke 11

The opportunity we miss most often is prayer.

It is the single largest, most powerful tool at our disposal, but too often we mumble a few words over our food and call it prayer.

What God wants is a relationship that lives and breathes prayer, because prayer is communication with God. It is seeking Him, desiring Him. Prayer is not just a list of requests that I make. It is a time of seeking His face, breathing in His presence, enjoying His Word, pouring out a heart of praise and thanksgiving and gratitude and love, and then opening up my heart to receive His love in return. Prayer is intimacy with the Creator. Prayer is the place where we can enter the Garden of Eden and walk and talk with God in the cool of the evening.

Prayer is not limited.

It is not limited by distance. No mile markers, no mountain ranges, no oceans can limit prayer. When I pray, I can come along side any work, in any location, in any culture. As quickly as a heartbeat, I can be a part of God's work around the world.

Prayer is not limited by finances. God has equipped each of us with funds and resources to give, and what a joy to be able to give and see God use those resources to empower the work around the world. But I can only give what I have. When I pray, I can ask God for the biggest, the best, the most to be accomplished for His Kingdom.

Prayer is not limited by talent, ability, intelligence, education or giftedness. I can join any ministry when I pray. I may not be able to sing a beautiful song, but I can join singers when I pray. I can join pastors, teachers, worship leaders, actors, people behind the scenes, and those very much in the forefront when I stand with them in prayer. There is no cultural, political, economic or language barrier that can limit prayer. Communism can't quiet it. Prison doors can't shut it out. The height of a career, the depth of sin, the pinnacle of power are no match for prayer.

Prayer is not limited by time. God is not limited to a schedule. He does not need a certain number of hours in a day to accomplish His plans. He does not need to make appointments.

Prayer is not limited because God is not limited and prayer is seeking God. He hears. He answers. He moves.

The opportunity we miss most often is prayer.

Luke 11:1-3. *"One day Jesus was praying in a certain place. When He finished, one of His disciples said to Him, 'Lord, teach us to pray, just as John taught His disciples.'*

He said to them, 'When you pray'..."

Day 19

Celebration Day

Psalm 146

"Praise the Lord. Praise the Lord, my soul..."

As you read Psalm 146 today, bless the Lord for His faithfulness.

Day 20

"Please send someone today to pray with me. I need help."

I had been praying, pleading with God over a situation. The burden was such a heavy one that I was having a hard time. I kept going back to the Lord but it sure felt like I needed someone to help me carry it for a little while. So one morning, when I was completely sunk under from the weight, I cried out to God and begged for Him to send someone to pray with me.

Then the normal duties called. I was trying to carry on with the routines even though that was hard.

Later that day there was a knock at the front door. Two ladies stood there. I knew them both. I had taught their children in school, had crossed paths with them at church functions. They were friends, but to my knowledge they had never been to my home. But on this day, my crying out to God for help day, here they were.

"We came today to pray with you." They had not come just for a visit. They had not come to get the inside details on the situation that was so heavy. They had come to pray. And they did. The three

of us prayed together for a while that day...a triple braided cord that was strong.

When they left, the situation and the pain were still there, but I knew that God had sent helpers to bring me into the presence of Jesus. He had heard my cry for help which meant He had also heard my burden. Instead of feeling weak, I felt so much stronger.

These friends, followers of the Lord, coming to help me enter into Christ's presence...what a gift.

Daniel 9

Daniel prayed. It's what he did and it's what he did often. Some people hated Daniel. They plotted and used his prayer life as a way to try to destroy him. He faced derision. He faced lions. He faced death to pray. When confronted with a challenge, he prayed. When he needed to understand, he prayed. When the understanding came, he prayed.

Sometimes he added fasting to his prayer life. Why would this man of prayer do that?

Fasting is sometimes a natural reaction to grief and distress. We see that with Daniel but also because he knew that it was not about less, it was about more. He was making more room in his life, more time in his day, more opportunities to spend with God.

Prayer defined Daniel's life.

So let's examine how Daniel prayed. Chapter nine is such a great model.

The first thing he did was to praise. Verse 4 *"Lord, the great and awesome God who keeps His covenant of love with those who love His commandments,"*

Secondly he confessed. Verses 5-6 *"...we have sinned and done wrong. We have been wicked and have rebelled; we have turned away from your commands and laws. We have not listened to your servants the prophets, who spoke in your name to*

*our kings, our princes and our ancestors and to all
the people of the land."*

Daniel continued his prayer, praising and confessing
his own sins and the sins of his people.

He knew his nation Israel needed help.

So he made his requests to God.

God saw his heart and that Daniel needed to hear
and see an answer.

Gabriel showed up. He instructed him by saying,
*"Daniel, I have now come to give you insight and
understanding. As soon as you began to pray, a
word went out that I have come to tell you, for you
are highly esteemed. Therefore consider the word
and understand the vision."* Daniel 9:22-23

Gabriel proceeded to relay to Daniel some amazing
insight into what was going to happen. It is so
precise, so exact that it is one of the many proofs
that the Bible is inerrant, infallible and completely
true. True then...true today! (Read Daniel 9:24-27.
This is history written in advance.)

So this pattern of prayer can be a model for us.
Praise, confess, request, and know that God hears
and is still answering, and then thank Him for that.

Day 21

The word *"wide"* makes us think open and free. Wide often denotes more instead of less. On the other hand the word *"narrow"* makes us think limited and restricted. It is a word that people associate with making their lives smaller not bigger.

But does narrow always mean less and is wide always a good choice?

When we were kids we played outside a lot. First of all we didn't have a great many inside toys. But we did seem to have lots of things to draw us outdoors. Hmmm, as I reflect on the reason for that, it suddenly occurs to me that it may have had more to do with having a little more quiet inside, if six kids were outside. So we had volleyball, basketball, tetherball, a swing set, a heavy duty rope swing, and a giant St. Bernard dog. Our dad couldn't just let him run. He would chase the horses and cows that lived next door to us. So Dad came up with a solution. King was tethered to a huge chain which was attached to a pulley. The pulley could slide along a thick cable giving him lots of room to run back and forth. His dog house was right smack in the middle of the run. It was a good set up for the dog since it was a huge, wide, open space.

But it was also the perfect place for a little activity we called *"Run through King's Pen."*

This was not a game. It was a test of survival. The object was to start on one side of the dog run and make it safely through all the obstacles. Since we were most often barefoot and this was one very large dog, there were definitely obstacles...brown piles of obstacles. (And I know you just love it when we refer to dog excrement.) We wanted to get all the way across to the other side without being caught by King. Yes, caught! King would run up, knock you down and get on top of you. Then it would be, *"Man down"* and the *"A Team"* would have to swoop in to rescue the victim. Even though sometimes as kids we fought with each other, we still lived by the code of honor *"Leave no man or kid behind"* in the danger zone.

And was it dangerous? The first time it happened to Kris, she fainted. Hysteria has a way of doing that.

Now in reality, this dog was a gentle giant. There wasn't a vicious bone in his gargantuan frame. He never bit, scratched or even growled. But it may have been the life saving techniques that were bred into his DNA that made him react the way he did if he caught you. Since St. Bernards have been used over the years to find people and keep them safe during blizzard conditions, it may have been only natural for King to want to protect. I'm sure it was with the best intentions that this massive, slobbering dog would knock you down to the ground and lay right on top of you, making sure you stayed warm and toasty even in the dead of summer.

So again, was it dangerous? Well, breathing is hard with that much dog flesh laying across your chest.

As for us, it didn't take us too many encounters to learn the safe zones within the dog run. Yet sometimes we pushed our limits, took chances. The element of danger was always there, so it drove us to see if we could get closer and still make it out safely. Invariably, in the very wide open space, we would find ourselves knocked down and covered over with a ton of dog fur, shoving to push his very large frame off of our very small ones and yelling for help.

But there was another area that offered a solution to the deep need for excitement.

We had a narrow hallway, probably too small today to get big pieces of furniture through. Narrow, empty hallway, seems mundane and limited doesn't it? But for us that narrow hallway was a chance to visit a place where few ever dared go. It was a chance to expand our horizons, head for the stars, well okay, the ceiling. You see if you went into that hallway barefoot and positioned your dirty feet and hands just right, you could literally climb the walls.

(We may have been the ones to coin that phrase.) You could inch your way all the way up and once there relax with your head touching the ceiling. It was uncharted territory, a foreign land, the final frontier, where no man, or kid, had gone before. I'm not sure who came up with this lofty idea first but once discovered, it was a place we often visited. I've heard astronauts say that space travel is hard to get out of your system. We agreed. We usually made the ascent though, when Mom was out in the garden and Dad was at work.

Since I'm pretty sure our parents never actually saw us climb the walls, I wonder if they ever had to ask themselves how dirty footprints got so close to the ceiling.

For us, wide offered danger, but narrow was a wonderful place just a little closer to heaven.

Matthew 7, John 10

Jesus said narrow was good. He said in Matthew 7:13 *"Enter through the narrow gate, for wide is the gate and broad is the road that leads to destruction, and many enter through it. But small is the gate and narrow the road that leads to life, and only a few find it."*

One road is wide. There's lots of room there for not only us, but also for all of those who encourage us to follow the crowd. And there is a crowd on that road. It's pretty popular and it almost looks like there's a party on that road. It's so easy to follow. We don't have to do much of anything except just be on it. But here's the thing that the party people don't want us to know, it leads to a precipice, a cliff. Someday when we cross over, we will fall right into the abyss.

Think about that for a moment. Jesus said that road leads to destruction. What if you were driving down a road and up ahead the bridge was out? If you knew that going over the cliff would lead to your death, would you turn around? Would you look for another way?

Jesus was telling us that there is a way, a path to follow that is not big or wide or popular. Some people believe that following this path will restrict their life. Nothing could be further from the truth. It is narrow, small. But it's small because we must enter through that gate alone. It's there that we meet Jesus. There's only room on that path for two. But Jesus Himself said in John 10:10 that it would lead to the biggest life. *"The thief comes only to steal, kill and destroy; I have come that they may have life, and have it to the full."*

LIFE! We can have life that is full, abundant, wonderful. That is what Jesus promises if we enter through His door, the one that looks narrow but leads to the biggest, most joyful life possible.

So here is the choice: the wide gate that leads to destruction, or the narrow one that leads to life.

Choose wisely.

Day 22

I spend a lot of time looking at the ground. Not because I want to necessarily but because little people can't tie shoes and I teach little people.

Most of the time, I don't mind tying shoes. It certainly isn't the most rewarding part of my job but it is necessary. The only time I have a real problem with it is when the kids come out of the bathroom and their shoelaces are wet. That is a call for the hand sanitizer, then hand washing and then hand sanitizer again. It can take a lot of time out of my day.

I always double tie the kid's shoes and sometimes triple tie them, but one of the great mysteries of the universe is how their shoes unravel from that. But they do and there I am again looking at the ground.

But I don't live there. My focus is not the ground. My focus is the kids.

There is not a lot to see when you just look down. I have never found gold or diamond rings or even much in the area of change. There just isn't much there. No, there isn't much beauty looking down.

So my focus is not the ground but the kids. When

I am done tying shoes, I get to look into their faces and joke with them that they owe me a million dollars for tying shoes. I get to see them laugh and run off to join their friends or go back to their work.

When I am done looking at the ground, I have the privilege of looking up.

Luke 13

She didn't have the privilege of looking up.

We don't know her name, or how old she was, or the color of her hair, or eyes. We don't know if she was rich or poor. We do know that she looked at the dirt.

Luke 13:10-17 tells us that she was a woman who was hunched over and couldn't stand up straight. She had been that way for eighteen years. She had spent eighteen years looking at other people's sandals and bare feet and the filth left behind by traveling animals.

She couldn't look into the faces of the crowd. Did the crowd ever really see her? Was she one of the invisible people unless she ran into them or they ran into her?

How fast can you move when you only look down? How do you get out of the way when you only look down?

How can you take a deep breath or laugh or even smile at someone?

It has to be a very lonely world much of the time looking at the dirt.

You see footprints in the sand, but do you ever see the mountains in the distance?

You might see darkness descending but can you see the sun rising?

You can see what is beneath you but can you see what is before you?

There isn't much to see when you can't look up.

But then Jesus saw her.

"On a Sabbath Jesus was teaching in one of the synagogues, and a woman was there who had been crippled by a spirit for eighteen years. She was bent over and could not straighten up at all. When Jesus saw her..." Luke 13:10-12

He saw her! She couldn't see Him, but He saw her.

What beauty there is in those words. What a startling revelation there is in those words. What an incredible message there is in those words. He saw her!

She was not invisible to Him. His eyes were on her.

She couldn't see much. He could see it all.

He called her forward.

For eighteen years her view had been the same. She had been bound to look at the dirt. It was a life that was less than ordinary. It was a life that saw the world as ugly and looked ugly to the world.

But then He called her forward because He saw her.

Her less than ordinary life was about to become more than extraordinary.

He spoke. He spoke freedom against her bondage. He laid both hands on her...loving, gentle, grace filled hands. Immediately she straightened up. Did she catch her breath? Did she laugh?

Did her eyes fill with tears?

She was set free. And what she saw first was the face of Jesus.

It seemed for eighteen years that her life was written in the dirt, but suddenly her life was written in eternity!

Day 23

And there was Alan.

Alan was a ball player. Good looking, athletic, charismatic, he was a popular kid. He filled his life with the stuff of high school. He was cool, accepted and lived just a little bit on the edge of the dangerous which made him more cool, more accepted.

As high school was winding down, he made a few choices that altered his path. Some choices do that.

Then he came to know Christ.

A new life, a new beginning, a clean slate...he could have relished this and savored it on his own.

But he didn't.

Almost as soon as he came to know Christ, Alan went to find his good friend. He wanted to tell him about the change in his life and that he could know Him too. The two sat in the driveway and Alan talked. He was so passionate, so on fire that his friend wanted to know Christ as well.

And then there were two...a team.

The two of them invited another friend on a trip to a ball game. It was an away game...far away. They both wanted this friend in the car so they could share about Christ uninterrupted. As they traveled the two young Christians told this third friend about a new life that he could have. By the time they were home this young man had also entered from death to life. The angels rejoiced...probably in three part harmony.

Alan's choices had led him down one path, but Jesus had more. This path was a calling to a life of sharing Him. Today Alan is a pastor.

You know he could have said, *"Sure I accepted Christ, but telling others about him? Well, that might make people uncomfortable. Getting my friends in the car with me and explaining that they are sinners in need of a Savior, well, that's not going to be a very popular message, and after all I was popular."*

But that isn't what Alan said. He wanted the guys he knew, his dear friends, to know his Best Friend and to have eternal life.

So he didn't care if his friends thought he was uncool. He didn't care if he made them feel a little uncomfortable as he talked. He didn't and doesn't care if people who hear his story think he's strange, or unpopular, or anything else. Alan doesn't care about the obstacles. He cares about the people.

Friends helping friends...Do you have a friend who needs help? Do you have someone who may need you to pray with them? Do you have a friend who needs to know Christ?

Does popularity, or status, or convenience really matter in the scope of eternity?

Mark 2

Their friend was bedridden, way more than just sick. He was paralyzed. Today a paraplegic or a quadriplegic can have special equipment. A person can be mobile. Although this is challenging and hard today, during the time of Christ it would have been really terrible. A paralyzed person would have been sentenced to a life of being prone on a mat, carried everywhere by others.

This man, this paralytic, had friends, good friends. They were the kind of friends who wanted this man to come to Jesus. So they took him. But when they got there the place was packed. It was more than standing room only. There wasn't even a way in, at least not until they looked up.

The roof may have been flat, most were. The Bible tells us it was tiled, not that easy to get through. It was designed to keep out...keep out rain, critters, robbers...keep out, not let in. We do know that these friends didn't care about the obstacles; they were determined to get this man to Jesus.

They climbed up. They started tearing up. They brought their friend up, and then right in the middle of Jesus' teaching, they lowered him down.

Friends bringing friends to Jesus...

Friends looking up to find a way to join someone who was weak to The One who is strong...

Friends not caring what the crowd thinks or even if it isn't popular to dig up a roof...

These friends had a mission.

"When Jesus saw their faith, he said to the paralyzed man, 'Son, your sins are forgiven.'" Mark 2:5

Did you catch what was said here? When Jesus saw THEIR faith, not only the paralyzed man's faith, He saw THEIR faith.

I love that. What it says to me is that God sees it when we go to pray with someone and join our faith with theirs, or when we share with someone about Jesus.

Of course what Jesus said was not popular with the religious leaders. It many times wasn't. But Jesus didn't care about popularity either.

"Now some teachers of the law were sitting there thinking to themselves, 'Why does this fellow talk like that? He's blaspheming! Who can forgive sins but God alone?' Immediately Jesus knew in His spirit that this was what they were thinking in their hearts, and He said to them, 'Why are you thinking these things? Which is easier to say to this paralyzed man, 'Your sins are forgiven,' or to say 'Get up, take up your mat and walk'? But I want you to know that the Son of Man has authority on earth to forgive sins.' So he said to the man, 'I tell you, get up, take your mat and go home.' He got up, took his mat and walked out in full view of

them all. This amazed everyone and they praised God, saying, 'We have never seen anything like this.'" Mark 2:8-12

These friends brought a man to Jesus and that man walked away changed.

Day 24

Lindy was late for church. She was a worship leader and she was running a bit behind for the early morning sound check. No time to stop and eat. She was part of the leadership. She set the example. If she wanted her team there on time, she had better be on time. So breakfast would have to wait, but as she drove she prayed. It was a very specific simple prayer.

"Lord, I'm hungry this morning, and I'm too late to stop and eat, so could You please somehow just send me a sausage biscuit? Thank You."

That was her prayer, a prayer for a sausage biscuit. Now Lindy actually could have waited to eat. She was not that hungry. She certainly could have gotten up earlier and had the time to stop for her own sausage biscuit, but as I said, she was running late.

Can I just tell you that I do not understand prayer? I do not know how it all works. But I do know that prayer is not getting God to do what we want. It is about a relationship with Him and in Luke 11, Jesus told us to ask. We can ask about big things and we can ask about little things.

Jesus told a story about a man who was not prepared for guests. So the man went to his neighbor in the middle of the night and asked for bread. The neighbor did not want to be bothered but because of the man's persistence the neighbor got up and got the bread. Jesus said to ask, to seek, to knock and keep on knocking, even if it's just about bread, or a sausage biscuit.

Lindy walked into church. One of our ushers, Harvey, was already there. He looked at Lindy and held out a bag. *"Lindy, for some reason today I bought two sausage biscuits and I have an extra one. Would you like it?"*

Would she like it? It was manna from heaven. It was miracle food. Please understand, Harvey was not in the habit of buying Lindy breakfast. This was the first and last time that he ever offered her a sandwich. It was not a ham and egg muffin, or even a sausage and cheese muffin. It was a sausage biscuit, the exact sandwich she had asked for. It was a miracle. The Great God of all creation had heard. He had answered the prayer of a twenty-something little girl who was a little bit hungry.

God answered a little prayer, but it was a huge miraculous answer. It wasn't parting of the Red Sea kind of big, but close, because it was God's immediate specific answer.

But it begs the question, *"Why would God send a sausage biscuit and not answer about the healing of a sick child, or free captives in prisons, or stop terrible awful inhumanity?"* I do not know, but I do know this. He has a purpose for the deep water. He has a purpose for the immediate answers. He has a purpose. I choose to trust.

Matthew 14

Prayer, taking our requests to God...no, I don't understand how it all works. But I do know the Scripture tells us in Philippians 4:6 *"Do not be anxious about anything, but in every situation, by prayer and petition, with thanksgiving, present your requests to God."*

We are to ask. But again, just because we ask does not mean God is going to answer in exactly the way we ask. Yet, we can rest in the fact that as we offer Him our requests, He offers us peace. Verse 7 continues, *"And the peace of God, which transcends all understanding, will guard your hearts and your minds in Christ Jesus."*

Peter asked...

Jesus told his disciples to get into the boat and go on ahead of Him to the other side of the lake.

Jesus went to pray, alone. The boat was out in the deep water, far from the land, and the winds were stirring up the waves, buffeting the boat.

They were in the storm. But Jesus always knows when there's a storm. He knew they were out there and He moved in closer to them.

"Shortly before dawn, Jesus went out to them, walking on the lake. When the disciples saw Him walking on the lake, they were terrified. 'It's a ghost,' they said, and cried out in fear. But Jesus

immediately said to them: 'Take courage! It is I. Don't be afraid.'" Matthew 14:25-27

The waves were crashing. The water was in turmoil. They were in the deep part of the lake, far away from land, and Peter made a request. He asked, *"Lord, if it is You...tell me to come to You on the water."* verse 28

An unusual request to say the least, Peter had been on the water many times, he was a fisherman. But he had never been ON the water without a boat underneath him.

And here in the midst of the storm, Jesus answered, *"Come."* verse 29

"Come"...such a simple answer. Such a mighty answer! In the terror of the night, in the middle of the sea, in the throes of the storm, an invitation, *"Come."*

Peter did. Against all reason, against all common sense, he got out of the boat and walked toward Jesus. What was impossible became possible and as long as he kept his eyes on the Savior, he stayed up. But even when the waves proved too scary and he faltered, Jesus was right there to catch him and get him back to the boat.

Are you going through a storm? Is there something that seems impossible? Or is there a simple request you would like to make? Jesus says, *"Take courage! It is I. Don't be afraid."* and then the invitation...*"Come."*

Day 25

I really do not like medical procedures. No, I am not just rambling. I hate them. And if you feel the same way, you can speed read over the next few sentences or even turn the page.

Don't get me wrong. I have the highest regard for all of those who have spent years preparing for this demanding, essential, life protecting, life-encouraging profession. I would just rather meet them at church than in their office. But there are times when there is little choice.

You see, I have a colonoscopy scheduled. When I scheduled this thing, I was not aware that there are rules to follow to get ready.

As I write this I am one week away from what I consider to be a walk through the valley of the shadow of death.

But in TWO days it will be Christmas! Starting today I have to go on a special diet and IN TWO DAYS it will be CHRISTMAS!

I can't eat seeds or red food dye or an undigested bit of beef or a fragment of an underdone potato. Wait! That is the argument that Scrooge waged against Marley as he faced death's door.

Am I facing death's door? Good question.

A medical team exploring the nearly twenty-eight feet of my innards kind of feels that way.

But back to my special and fun diet. It means no pecan pie or cookies with nuts or red beets. (Well, I am probably okay with the beet one.) But I can't eat strawberries or tomatoes or most of my favorite candy. Are you weeping with me yet?

This goes on for a week but then, now get this, I have to skip the morning coffee the day of the procedure. This is a day when I could have sat in my favorite chair, my feet propped up, coffee in hand, for as long as I wanted. Give up coffee? Where did that come from?

And on top of all that there is some kind of prep that I will have to drink that is supposed to leave me as sparkling on the inside as I am on the outside. As jarringly surprising as it sounds, this prep proclaims no refills. Can you imagine?

The last time I did this was about twenty years ago and I had to throw away the glass I had been using to drink the swill because every time I looked at it, I gagged. Boy, am I ever looking forward to this!

I told you that I hate medical procedures. It is for these very reasons that it has taken me twenty years to schedule my second one!

Now the hospital assured me that they would put me to sleep but the last time I had this procedure I had to do the whole thing without any meds. Apparently I gave them some signal that I was having a reaction. I think it was because I started to retch.

Yep, fun day ahead.

So why am I doing this?

I need to know if I am as light as a feather or as merry as a school girl...sorry, Scrooge again.

This is what I am asking: *"Am I healthy?"*

It is an age-old question. I personally don't go there that often but there are times to visit. Occasionally I have to look ahead and wonder. *"Am I okay?"*

There is a reason that question is asked, not just by me, but by most of us. It is because I was born to live...but am bound to die. It is true of all of us. And we know it. Yes, it is true of all of us...except One.

He was born to die but was bound to live.

And that changes everything.

Daniel 1, 10

I am going to revisit something that is a little un-usual and a lot misunderstood. It is called *"fasting."* It is a very Biblical concept but nowhere does it say that it is something that we must do. Nowhere does it say that there is only one way or one purpose behind fasting.

A lot of people think that fasting just means that you have to give something up. Does it?

There are things that are easy to give up. I could easily say that I am going to give up eating liver. Not one day would go by for the rest of my life and I would be sorry I had declared that as a part of a fast.

It wouldn't bother me to never eat raw fish or the green stuff in a lobster that once helped him breathe or any kind of animal organ meat or colonoscopy prep!

I know a young woman who is pregnant with her second child. She sent a text to her mom that read: *"The girl in the cubicle next to me just heated up Brussels sprouts. I may have to kill her!"* I am guessing that she could give those up pretty easily right now.

There are things that don't mean that much to me that I could eliminate from my diet. It isn't that I don't like them, but I can certainly get along without them. I can give up licorice, lima beans, kale, macaroni and cheese, bagels. I could make a long list but you get my point.

But then there are things that I have a terrible time giving up...COFFEE! Well, that might be the toughest one.

Giving up things? Is that what it means to fast?

What should I look like when I fast? Disheveled? Grief stricken? Wearing sackcloth? Sitting in ashes? Should I weep or whimper or sob or smile or laugh? Should I tell people? Do I wrap up the cheeseburger someone just brought me, shove it in my pocket and let the cheese ooze leaving grease spots on my new jeans?

What does it mean when someone goes on a Daniel fast? Who is Daniel and what kind of fast is that?

Where is the book of rules on fasting? What outlet store carries sackcloth and ashes and where do I get Daniel's food?

So let's unpack this.

First of all, fasting is not nearly as much about giving up as it is about making room. I can give up a little sleep so I have room for a little more time with the Lord in the morning. I can give up some of the hours of prep time cooking fabulous meals. (Wait, who is writing this? I am the sister with the reputation for bad cooking so where does all the prep time come in? Well, for me it might be more cleanup time from all of the messes I make cooking.) Whatever the case, replace the time and make it count with the Lord.

Microwaving a potato doesn't take nearly as much time as preparing lasagna. Eating an apple is far simpler than making the pie. Fasting can mean making room for something that is more important.

Sometimes fasting comes because we have no other choice. When we walk through the valley of the shadow of death, some of us can't eat. We can't even swallow. We don't have to look like we are grieving. We are grieving. We don't have to buy sackcloth because everything we put on looks like it came out of a stall and the hurt or pain is so much that we don't even care. The face is ashen, the heart is breaking. We find those kinds of fasts in the Bible.

In Daniel 10, we see Daniel acting that way. He is so overcome that he can hardly eat. He may not have even bathed. He is broken. His response is to pray.

But in Daniel 1, his fasting comes from a different motivation. Daniel is being asked to eat food that does not meet the standards that God had outlined in His Word. Every rule that He gave them was for their protection and for His name to be known throughout the world. Their obedience was to help other nations to see the joy, freedom, health, peace, and rest that God wanted the world to experience. I am going to take a rabbit trail for a moment, so walk it with me. Many people say that the Bible is just a bunch of rules. Really? Let me give you a count. There are exactly 613.

How many tax laws or traffic laws or zoning laws or clean air...do I need to continue? We have so many laws in this country that literally you can't count them all. It can make your head swim and we don't want that because I think we have laws about heads swimming. There are only 613 in God's Word and each one can be put under a heading...Love God. Love people. They are all there for our peace, rest and restoration.

So back on track...In Daniel 1:8 he is told that he has to break some of God's rules about food. He can't. He knows it is dangerous to say *"No"* to a king who had a reputation for gouging out people's eyes and burning down temples. But Daniel cared more about what God thought than he cared about what the king thought. What a wonderful way to live!

Daniel didn't march in there like a storm trooper, with his arms crossed and *"No way Nebuchadnezzar"* on his lips.

He put together a plan.

I think he prayed about it before he ever spoke it. He asked if he and his friends could try something. He wanted to eat fruits, vegetables, grains and water for ten days and to see where that would land them. It wasn't long enough to do much harm but it was long enough to make a difference. And what a difference it made! At the end of ten days, Daniel and his friends were stronger, smarter and better looking than all of the other young men.

There are different directions that a fast can take. One way can be considered a complete fast, only drinking water. Another way is to only eat a plant-based diet and that is what we see in Daniel 1 and 10. In chapter 1 it was ten days and in chapter 10 he fasted for twenty-one days. Yes, there were some things that he gave up. It was not nearly as much about what he gave up, but rather about what he gained and that was time with the Lord.

Fasting can be a wonderful way to deepen our walk with Jesus.

Remember that this is not meant to be bondage about what you can eat and what you can't. It is not meant to create a platform for judgment that speaks condemnation because someone isn't following your exact plan. This is to allow you to rest from the pressure of food and find rest in the presence of Jesus. It is a chance to let your body rest from a lot of those things that slow you down. Face it, a big hunk of chocolate cake has a tendency to create a bit of a sludgy feeling.

And who knows? At the end of a season of fasting and prayer, you may be stronger, smarter and better looking than you have ever been. I wonder if that might be because you are going to spend more time in the mirror of God's Word and more time looking into His face than yours.

So grab a cup of your favorite plant-based water (Remember no judgment on anyone for the way they approach this.) and make some room for Jesus.

I have to wonder. What might happen in our churches if we walked into a worship experience with a hunger for the banquet of His Word and a calling to pray instead of calling our favorite restaurant?

It is something to pray about.

Day 26

Celebration Day

Psalm 147

"Praise the Lord. How good it is to sing praises to our God."

If you are beginning a fast, applaud the Lord for His sustaining power.

Day 27

She knew she was in labor. She knew. She wasn't second-guessing. This wasn't false labor. She knew she wasn't going to get to the hospital and have them say, *"Oh no, Honey, not yet!"* She knew because her water had broken that morning and this was her body's gentle way of saying, *"GET TO THE HOSPITAL!"*

She was an RN and knew that a team of doctors and nurses, her friends and colleagues, were on call waiting for this delivery because she was having triplets. She knew this was a first for her obstetrician, pediatrician and for the hospital. It was definitely her first.

She knew she wasn't supposed to eat. She knew she should really limit even how much water she drank. Did I say, SHE WAS A REGISTERED, CERTIFIED, FULLY QUALIFIED, WELL TRAINED NURSE? She had assisted in labor rooms. She had helped with deliveries. She had worked the maternity ward. She knew the rules and yet here she was eating. She knew that there was a way better than slight chance that the lovely lunch she was now swallowing, she was going to meet again coming back up and it wouldn't be lovely.

Mom knew.

I doubt Dad could even swallow. He was probably in the car with the motor running.

Her reason? This was home. It was Easter and Grandma had cooked Easter dinner. More than just a Sunday lunch, this was a banquet for the holiday, roast chicken, mashed potatoes, dessert, etc. Mom was hungry and it was Easter and she wanted to eat. So she waited and she ate and she feasted.

And finally she thought she had better get to the hospital. When they arrived, Dad could finally breathe and swallow and sit upright. Dad was not good with hospital stuff and usually met medical emergencies in the prone position.

Mom wanted the banquet. She wanted the feast. She wanted the food and the fellowship. She had a really good reason to miss the feast, she had babies to deliver. But because she wanted to eat, she chose the feast.

A few short hours later at 5:00 in the afternoon we started arriving, three little babies, tiny by normal standards, but not so bad for three.

Today all of us love to feast on special days...I guess we got it naturally.

Luke 14

The banquet was ready...the guests were not.

The invitations went out. The table was elaborately set. The food was meticulously prepared. The host's home was exquisite. The invitation showed such honor to each recipient. This gracious host simply wanted to share all the beauty of his home, all the abundance of his table, all the splendor of his wealth with his guests.

The great banquet was ready. The servant went to the home of each invited guest so they were sure to know they were wanted. It was the custom. First send the invitation and then follow up by sending the servant with a gentle call, *"Come, for everything is now ready."*

Who wouldn't want to come? It was, after all, a banquet. The food would be plentiful and delicious. The fellowship would be sweet and satisfying, the beautiful surroundings restful to the soul. Who wouldn't say, *"Yes"*?

The banquet was ready... the guests were not.

"But they all alike began to make excuses. The first said, 'I have just bought a field, and I must go and see it. Please excuse me.' Another said, 'I have just bought five yoke of oxen, and I'm on my way to try them out. Please excuse me.' Still another said, 'I just got married, so I can't come.'" Luke 14:18-20

The banquet was ready; they were not. Their lives got in the way of the most important occasion in all of life.

They missed the banquet.

They missed the feast, the fellowship, the beauty, the splendor. They missed their opportunity and for what? A field, a cow, a little time!

So the host called in the servant, *"Go out quickly into the streets and alleys of the town and bring in the poor, the crippled, the blind and the lame."* Luke 14:21

So when the invitation arrived he couldn't believe it. There must be some mistake. His name must have gotten confused with someone else. This was A-list stuff, certainly not his crowd. This invitation was for the elite of the town, not the down and out. Not him. This had to be a mistake.

He was dirt poor and dirty, lame and crippled. He could read people's opinion of him in their faces. Most overlooked him, but for those who dared, it was disdain, disgust or once in a while a modicum of pity. They knew he didn't belong. He knew he didn't belong. Everyone in town looked down on him. He most certainly would not be welcome here.

But the invitation had his name. Why not just go for a few moments and see? Why not just get a whiff of the glorious food? Why not catch a glimpse of the celebs and elite who actually belonged there?

Yes, he would go and see and smell and take a deep breath and breathe it all in and enjoy it for one breathtaking moment, before they recognized their mistake and threw him out. He would feast on that moment for the rest of his life.

So he said, *"Yes"*. He went.

Trembling, waiting for the rebuke he was sure to come for his audacity, he saw all the magnificent beauty. He smelled the delicious food; he felt the sweetness of the fellowship.

And then the host saw him. He waited for the recriminations. He waited for the harsh look and the caustic rebuke that he, with his dirt and sin, had dared to say yes to the invitation.

But there was no rebuke, just love, pure joy on his host's face, *"Welcome, welcome!"* He felt perfectly at home.

And then suddenly a realization, he didn't just feel at home. HE WAS HOME.

Day 28

Shalom

We translate the word as peace. Shalom does mean peace, but it is a big word with an even bigger meaning. It is more than just lack of war. It is bigger than just freedom from conflict. Shalom is what God offers to us.

Let me try to illustrate with words what cannot really be put into words.

You are in a big luxurious cabin in the mountains. The snow is falling furiously outside, but the blazing fire in the huge stone fireplace is warm and inviting. The mantel is decorated with lovely pine greenery along with a few red berries and colored lights which send out a welcome glow. A delicious soup is simmering away on the back burner of the stove and homemade bread is baking in the oven. The smell of the freshly baking bread lends its sweet scent to the heavenly smell of the pine in the room. You sit with feet propped up and a cup of steaming hot chocolate. This isn't from one of those envelopes of cocoa mix, but rather real chocolate shavings that transform a hot cup of milk into a silken indulgence. Marshmallows float on top and it's stirred with a candy cane. Oh, and you aren't even worried about the calories.

Every bit of your work is finished. There are no pressing appointments that call to you, no worrisome presentations to prep for, no phone calls to get back to, the work is all done.

As the snow falls outside you can watch deer and elk and buffalo come close to the gigantic picture window. Music plays in the background and a really good book rests by your side.

Perhaps I forgot to mention, this is not a vacation place, but the place where you live. This is home.

This is but a small picture of shalom. This is the peace, the shalom that Jesus offers when He says to come and He will give us rest, or when He says He has peace to offer that the world doesn't know. It is the place you can enter when you feast on His presence.

He did all the work so we could enter into the rest and peace, the shalom that He offers.

Luke 15

"Jesus continued: 'There was a man who had two sons. The younger one said to his father, 'Father, give me my share of the estate.' So he divided his property between them.'" Luke 15:11-12

Theirs was a prominent family. They had all the amenities that wealth could afford, servants, land, livestock, nice clothes, plenty to eat. Theirs was the home people envied living in. But growing up in such a home, the two sons took for granted their lot in life. Wealth, prosperity, it was due them. Then, as children sometimes do, the younger son became weary of the old man. Family responsibilities were tedious and the world looked so inviting. Surely there was more to life than helping with the estate, working in the fields and dinner with Dad.

The boy went to his father, *"Father, give me my share of the estate."* Luke 15:12a

The father would have known exactly what that meant. Estates were not divided until the father died, but Dad wasn't accommodating him. This father was living too long to suit his child. This ungrateful son didn't want a relationship. He wanted the money. He didn't want fellowship. He wanted all that the father's wealth could buy. He didn't want the father; he wanted the father's possessions.

"So he divided his property between them."
Luke 15:12b

Well, he now had it. He had all of it. The coins jingled in his pockets and their tune sang freedom... freedom. No more early days of working in the fields along with the servants. No more late night dinners with the family, listening to Dad's boring old stories.

He could party. He could feast. He could drink. He could do whatever he wanted. And so he did. Riotous, wild living and he paid the bill. Ah yes, this was the life he had longed for, perhaps a little less satisfying then he had thought, but still, he had friends and fun and he was now the master of his fate. Day after day, week after week, and suddenly...it was gone. Gone! The money was gone, his inheritance spent, and with it, gone were all his *"friends."*

And then a severe famine. Nothing grew, nothing prospered, nothing to eat. This terrible awful famine was in the country, but it was also in his soul. He had nothing. He had no one. He had no place to turn. He took the only job he could find. He hired himself out to slop and tend pigs. PIGS! His family didn't raise pigs. He hadn't realized how dirty and stinking these animals were.

But he was starving and the slop and swill he was feeding these stinking creatures was looking good to him. He longed to eat the pig's food. And then he knew. What had promised freedom had only brought bondage. The lifestyle that had looked so good on the outside was bitter inside. This life that he had longed for was NOT the life he wanted. But the hunger in his stomach was nothing compared to the hunger, the longing in his heart.

Home...his father...his family...HOME! At home even the servants had life so much better. But he could never go home; he had burned too many bridges. And yet, a servant? Maybe...maybe?

Luke 15:17 *"When he came to his senses, he said, 'How many of my father's hired servants have food to spare, and here I am starving to death!'"*

"When he came to his senses..." This son thought about home, the warmth of the fire on a cold night, his father's stories, the laughter, tables laden with food, the warmth of his father's embrace. Just a short time ago it had all seemed so lackluster, so drab and boring. Now his heart nearly broke with longing for it. Of course at home he had done his share of the work, working in the fields, right alongside the servants, but in the evening, he came into the dining room for dinner. During the day he might have felt like a servant, but always at night he knew the difference...he was the son.

Now, however, his own choices had made him the servant, a slave. He was just a nameless, faceless servant to a man who couldn't care less about him. His father never treated his servants like this.

Home...he would never be welcome again as a son. His share in that was now long gone. He had squandered it all in extravagant waste. There was no going back to the life of a son. But what if he went to his father and asked to be a servant? He would work. He would slave for the rest of his life to just be allowed to see his father's face again.

And so he settled it in his heart. He would turn around, go back home, beg his father's forgiveness, and plead for the privilege of serving him.

All the way home he thought about what he could say. Certainly he could never justify his horrendous behavior. He was without excuse, except for his own selfishness and sinfulness.

"Father, I have sinned against heaven and against you. I am no longer worthy to be called your son: make me like one of your hired servants."
Luke 15:18-19.

Still a long way from home, his heart beat wildly with fear. How would his father react? What scathing words might he say? His father had every right to turn him away. The hurt and pain, the shame he had brought to his father, he deserved nothing but scorn and derision and rebuke.

Day 29

Birthdays are supposed to be times to celebrate.
Even twenty-nine, thirty-nine, forty-nine and holding
can be celebrations. You have a party, go out to
dinner, put the diet on the shelf, have a cake and
eat it too. Celebrations.

It was for one of those birthdays that we were
supposed to go out to dinner. We had called Karen
and John. (Hopefully by now you have a firm grasp
on the fact that we are four sisters who are telling
our stories and not one person with a personality
disorder that screams of a very deluded female!)
We scheduled to go out to dinner to turn another
year older and another year wiser.

But Dave called.

I can't even begin to calculate the number of times
that sentence has been tacked onto my plans.

Ready to walk out the door and Dave calls.
Ready to sit down to dinner and Dave calls.
But this was my birthday and Dave called.

Now I have a choice. I can be angry, kick furniture,
scream, cry. There are a lot of options and I have
lived them all. I spent the first seven years of my

married life doing all of the above because my plans were interrupted because Dave called. Or sometimes because Dave didn't call. I can't even begin to count the number of times I had him dead and buried because he was supposed to come home and wasn't there. Surely he must be dead or he would have called me.

Now I am going to stop the flow of my story and give you a little insight into my husband. People can be lumped into all kinds of categories. You can group by age, race, color of hair. The list can go on and on. But the one that has caused Dave and me the most trouble over the years is the *"event"* vs. *"time"* orientation.

Let me explain. I am time oriented. There is a little clock that ticks off in my head that tells me when a certain amount of time has passed. It makes me know that it is time to check my watch because I have to be somewhere. It means that I was able to get my kids to school on time, pick them up on time and keep them on some kind of reasonable schedule that included doing homework, going to bed, getting up in the morning. Through the years any tardiness on the kids' report cards was not my doing! If I say I will be somewhere at a certain time, I am usually there...early!

Dave, however, is event oriented. It means that whatever is happening right in front of him is what is important and everything else can wait. He has very little concept of time. It works great if I happen to be the event but not so good if the rest of the world is. And much of the time I have not been the event.

So I spent the first seven years of our married life angry, crying, frustrated because I really could not understand this. I tried to change him but do you know what I have discovered? I have no ability to change Dave. But God does. So I finally decided I would ask the Lord to change Dave. And the changes started to take place. It was almost miraculous. I stopped having to get angry or crying or planning his funeral. The changes began and I could breathe again after seven long years.

Oh, wait, did I tell you that God didn't change him?

God changed me.

I had asked God to fix Dave. Instead, God in His grace began to fix me.

I have said this before and I am going to say it again but this time I am going to say it in capital letters. I AM NOT SUPER SPIRITUAL!

It often takes a very long time for me to get a message. But I finally started to listen.

I wanted Dave to come home on time. The Lord

told me to give Dave's schedule over to Him.

I wanted Dave to spend more time with me. The Lord told me He wanted me to spend more time with Him.

I wanted Dave to put me in front of everyone else. The Lord told me that He wanted Dave to put Him before everyone else and that included me.

I'm not going to give you the whole list, I am going to sum this up by saying that He told me that my life is not my own. My expectations are to be turned over to Him and to trust Him for my life. He is my source.

You are probably thinking that I left myself wide open to being a widow with a living husband!

And you would be right, I did.

But God's plan for a marriage is not *"married singles"* living two totally different lives. God wants a man and woman to marry and become one. That is pretty tough to accomplish when you are mad all the time.

I let go. I got out of the way and Jesus took over.

People started coming to Dave and telling him to go home.

Four tickets were placed in Dave's hand for our family to spend twelve days in Hawaii, all expenses paid. The only catch? He couldn't take any work.

We were given a condo in the Cayman Islands for a week. This setting was so lovely that a movie production company had approached the family about using it as a possible setting for their film. On top of the place to stay, they left us gift cards to their favorite island restaurants.

We have had dear friends who have given us time every summer to sit in the beauty of their beachfront condo and do nothing but rest. It has been a retreat that allows us to breathe salt air, catch our breath and catch up on where we are headed as a couple.

Are you catching what I am saying? I let go and Jesus took over.

So back to my birthday. Dave called to tell me that he had just been asked to go to the home of a dying woman. It would mean that he was going to be late to go out to dinner. I knew it might mean that he wouldn't make it home in time at all.

Was I angry? I can tell you that I wasn't. My life is not about my schedule. I can make myself a sandwich and we can go out another time. I called Karen and John and told them to go on ahead.

It was a little while but Dave finally got home. He had a story to tell.

When he reached the woman's house, this dear lady had called her entire family to gather around her. She was still able to talk so she introduced Dave, not as much by name but as her pastor. She told her family that he was the one who had explained to her how she could invite Jesus into her life, be forgiven of all of her sins, and know for certain that she was on her way to heaven. She asked him to explain that to her family and for all of them to invite Christ into their lives. In her last moments she wanted them to understand the Gospel. In those few minutes, her family heard and responded. They wanted to know Jesus too.

Yes, Dave got home in time so we could go out to dinner.

But he had gotten to her home in time so her family could go to heaven.

You tell me which one mattered the most!

Luke 15

The father paced. He walked. He scanned the horizon.
He looked again, on and on, day after day, willing
his son to come home, but little believing that he
would. They had not parted on the best terms.
When the boy came and demanded his share of the
estate, it was as if the old man's breath had been
kicked out of him, not sure he would ever breathe
again. The realization, the pain of what the boy was
asking broke his heart, stole moments from his life.
The family he thought he had was not real. The boy
had no love for his father. He only loved what the
old man had. The reality was gut wrenching.

But, this father had enough love for them both. His
love never wavered for his wayward child. His boy
was away from home, away from protection, away
from shalom, away from his father's love. And so it
went, day after day, week after week, looking, waiting,
praying, hoping, willing his boy to come home.

And then, off in the distance, a familiar gait, a form
he knew well, had watched grow. His son was
walking toward home. The old man began to run,
undignified, indeed shameful in this culture, for any
male in a flowing robe, but more so for an old, old
man. He didn't care. In fact, he welcomed the
gossip's eyes on him. He would take the shame
away from the boy and onto himself. Let the
neighbors laugh at him, scorn his behavior. Darkness
turned to light; death was swallowed up in life. His
son had come HOME!

"The son said to him. 'Father I have sinned against heaven and against you. I am no longer worthy to be called your son.'

But the father said to the servants, 'Quick! Bring the best robe and put it on him. Put a ring on his finger and sandals on his feet. Bring the fattened calf and kill it. Let's have a feast and celebrate. For this son of mine was dead and is alive again; he was lost and is found.' So they began to celebrate."
Luke 15:21-24

When the older son came near the house, he heard music. Music? Dancing? There had been no celebrating in this house for a very long time. He called a servant, "What's going on?"

The servant answered in verse 27, "Your brother has come. Your father has killed the fattened calf because he has him back safe and sound."

Furious, the older boy refused to go in. The father came to him and pleaded with him to come in too. The banquet, the feast was ready, "Come in."

Verse 29: "But he answered his father, 'Look! All these years I've been slaving for you and never disobeyed your orders. Yet you never gave me even a young goat so I could celebrate with my friends.'"

I...I...I

Good deeds aside, the son had come to a place of decision. Would he say *"Yes"* to the father's offer? We are not told his answer.

There are two sons, the unrighteous, and the self-righteous. Both are loved dearly. The father comes to each with the offer of feasting, celebrating, rejoicing in the father's house. But each one must make his own decision. The offer is for us as well. What stops us? Is it the lure of the world, or our pride and trust in our own righteousness that keeps us from saying *"Yes"* to the Father's invitation to come.

Day 30

It was the doctor's job to deliver the truth, and the truth was that the man had cancer. And the truth in this case was that it was terminal. He had a short time to live. And so, in as kind a way as he could possibly say it, the doctor informed the patient.

The doctor received a call telling him that he had really devastated this terminally ill man with the news. But whether the patient wanted to hear it or not, the truth was he was dying. Now there are always miracles. This doctor believes in miracles, has probably seen a fair share, but he has also witnessed cancer, like a python, squeeze the life out of someone. Since time began, since Adam and Eve ate the fruit, death has reigned in our world. But death does not necessarily mean defeat.

The doctor made a house call and went to talk to the man.

This physician asked a simple question, *"Are you thinking you might soon be standing before God, and are there a few things that you think are pretty big that you have done?"*

"Yes," the ill man acknowledged.

"Have you ever murdered someone?"

Well, no, he hadn't.

The doctor began to tell a Bible story:

"A man named Saul in the Bible was a murderer. He worked hard to imprison Christians and even helped to kill a believer named Stephen, whose only crime was believing that Jesus was the Messiah. So this Saul was a pretty bad guy by our standards, a murderer. But Jesus came to Saul. Jesus Himself appeared to him, knocked him off his horse and gently spoke words of salvation to Saul. And you know what? Saul believed the Lord and received the gift of salvation. Saul became Paul and helped pen a great portion of the New Testament. He started churches. He shared the Good News, lots of people became Christians. He was imprisoned for his faith and eventually died as a martyr. From pretty bad to greatly used, a real hero, God did it all. And God can and will do that for anyone."

(You can read Paul's story in the book of Acts. It is pretty amazing stuff.)

And then the doctor asked a third question. *"Would you like to receive God's gift of salvation?"*

This dying man said, *"Yes!"*

And with a prayer of commitment this critically ill man went from dying to eternal life.

The very next day he breathed his last breath here, but breathed heavenly air there. Jesus, the bridegroom, came to carry him across death's threshold into a brand new life.

I'm sure his death was devastating for those who loved him, but it wasn't a devastating death. This was a glorious death because Jesus came to save this one sinner, and to save all sinners, all who will receive Him, no matter what we've done.

A very caring physician led a very dying man to the very Great Physician.

Luke 16

Jesus told a story: *"There was a rich man who was dressed in purple and fine linen and lived in luxury every day."* Luke 16:19

There lived a rich man. This rich man had it all. He was rich, no question about it. Money was no object. If he didn't already own something, he had the cash. Clothes? His were the finest. He dressed in purple, the color of royalty. He wore the finest linen, soft and beautiful. He looked every bit his elevated station in life. He dined on the most gourmet meals his chefs could prepare. His were the finest cuts of meat, the richest of desserts. He grew fat on the abundance. He lived in luxury. His home was in a gated community. He was set apart from the riffraff of society.

His life was a dream.

"At his gate was laid a beggar named Lazarus, covered with sores and longing to eat what fell from the rich man's table. Even the dogs came and licked his sores." Luke 16:20-21

There lived a poor man named Lazarus. He had nothing at all. Lazarus was not just poor, but a destitute beggar. Day after day he was laid outside of this rich man's gate to beg. Clothes? His were nothing but rags. Lazarus was malnourished and sick. Dogs licked the blood oozing from his sores. He longed to eat the few crumbs that fell from the rich man's table.

His life was a nightmare.

But death makes no distinction. It came for both.

The rich man ended up in torment. Lazarus was carried into eternal life.

Now let me interject something lest we think that denial and insufficiency are the path to heaven. They are not. Neither do riches and abundance keep someone out of heaven. The Bible tells us that we are all sinners. We all need the Savior. The issue is not riches or the lack of them, the issue is the Savior. If money and abundance keep someone from recognizing that they need Jesus, then the riches are worthless. If need and insufficiency help someone recognize that they must be born again, then insufficiency is worth it.

Whether rich or poor, simply stated, we all need the All Sufficient One.

Day 31

We put her on the plane. It was not easy. She was the child I never dreamed would go, but was the one God chose to go. As a little girl she cried and worried if her dad and I had to be away. She cried with the baby sitters. She always wanted kids to visit us overnight, but she did not want to spend the night away from home. So I didn't see it coming when she said she thought God was calling her to a country in Europe for at least a year. She sent in her application to the mission board even though the deadline for applications had already passed. They accepted her.

She had to raise support, and she had less than three months to do it. Three months to raise what seemed an exorbitant amount of money. It could NOT be done. She sold her car, she cashed in some savings, the family pledged monthly support, but it was not nearly enough. She made phone calls, set up meetings and shared her call to go and people did give, but it was still not enough. She had such a short amount of time. It really was not possible.

But if God wants a door open, it opens. People started calling us, *"I hear that Joy is raising support for a mission trip. I want to help."*

In three tiny months she had every bit of her support. We knew God had done it.

We knew this was where the girl was supposed to be. When we put her on a plane all by herself, her dad and I cried and cried. She sobbed as she went. We did not know it would be so hard, but she got on the plane because that was where God wanted her, and we went home without our child. It was hard. But she had a job to do; she was to go and tell. We had a job to do; our job was to stay and pray.

Several months in she called. The team needed God's direction. They were planning to fast for a season and engage people back home to pray for an hour a day for the next forty days.

Joy asked if I would be on her team. Are you kidding? I was already on the team. I absolutely said, *"Yes!"* I would love to pray for an hour a day for the country where God had called my girl.

I was in. I rose early the next day, an extra hour to pray.

But saying yes to pray is different from praying. I set the timer for one hour and began to pray. *"Oh God, please bless this country where you called my girl..."* That said, now what was I going to pray about for the next 59 minutes and 55 seconds? One hour seemed impossible.

I opened my Bible. I was taking a class on Matthew and we were in Matthew 13. I began to read the parable of the sower.

Suddenly I knew. The seed was being sown. The team was there sharing. The soil was what needed to be prayed for, the hearts of the people. God showed me that from the country's leaders to the beggars on the street, I was to pray for as many of those individuals as I could think of. Political leaders, school teachers, moms and dads, college and high school kids, little ones, all the people, all walks of life, I took the hearts of the people to the heart of God and suddenly the timer went off.

I knew God had given me the path to pray for this country.

A few days later Joy sent me an email. *"Mom, here's the Scripture we are using over the next forty days. It is Matthew 13, the parable of the sower."*

I wept as I saw the miracle. God had united a team across the miles. His plan, not ours, what a joy it was to get to be a part of it.

Matthew 13

"That same day Jesus went out of the house and sat by the lake. Such large crowds gathered around Him that He got into a boat and sat in it, while all the people stood on the shore. Then He told them many things in parables, saying..."
Matthew 13:1-3

Jesus told stories. Jesus used the everyday to tell us about the eternal. The stories He told are just as viable today as they were two thousand years ago. They are still just as meaningful.

Matthew 13 is the parable of the sower. It begins:

"A farmer went out to sow his seed. As he was scattering the seed, some fell along the path, and the birds came and ate it up. Some fell on rocky places, where it did not have much soil. It sprang up quickly, because the soil was shallow. But when the sun came up, the plants were scorched, and they withered because they had no root. Other seed fell among thorns, which grew up and choked the plants. Still other seed fell on good soil, where it produced a crop—a hundred, sixty or thirty times what was sown. Whoever has ears, let him hear."
Matthew 13:3-9

A simple little story about a farmer, but filled with challenges for us.

What kind of soil are we? Are we shallow with little

depth to our lives? Do the things of life like money, work or worries choke out our relationship with the Lord? Are we letting our roots grow deep into the Word? Are we producing a crop? Does anyone know the Lord better because they can see Jesus in our lives?

Jesus told the story then, but it still is for us today. So what kind of soil are we?

Day 32

Are you a pastor? Do you know a pastor? Would you like to be a pastor?

Are you a pastor's wife? Do you know a pastor's wife? Would you like to be a pastor's wife?

I grew up thinking this was a pretty easy job. You got to live in a church provided home. You visited a little in the hospital. You studied to preach a sermon or two each week. You were invited to people's homes for dinner and then sat on their porches and drank lemonade until time to go home. Life seemed simple and orderly and had a little halo that stretched around the pastor's family because they were doing such important work. It seemed to me that it had a certain glory and blessing around it that made it pure joy to face the world. I decided early in life that I wanted to be a pastor's wife. And the biggest perk of all? Surely you would know that you were going to heaven. Of course pastors and their families had to get in. I was pretty certain that rule had been written in stone somewhere.

I couldn't have been more wrong. Yes, being in the ministry can be rewarding. It can be a tremendous blessing to get to serve in that way. But make no mistake; life in the ministry is life in the trenches. It can be dirty and messy and inconvenient and hurtful and hard.

I am a pastor's wife.

For a little while we lived in a church owned home. I was expected to keep it clean and neat and at any time people could drop by and use my house. One Sunday after church, a girl who had not headed home after the service yet, rang my doorbell and almost shoved her way in. *"I have to use the bathroom!"*

"Okay, it's just down the hall."

She didn't make it. She didn't tell me that. She just left and I discovered I now had a carpet shampoo party ahead of me for the day.

We had a youth meeting at our house one Sunday afternoon. As the day got later, I knew I needed to get ready for the evening service. I ran into our bedroom, shut the door and ducked into the bathroom...didn't bother to close the bathroom door. I had turned on the bathroom light but not the bedroom until I decided to check my make-up before the service.

As soon as I turned on the light, I saw him. A guy was sleeping in our bed. I guess he had gotten tired and since it wasn't really my home he could sleep anywhere he wanted. This event is on the top ten list of the maddest I have ever been. I headed straight to my husband, interrupted what he was doing and demanded that he get him out of our room! There was not one ounce of grace in me. I wanted to hurt the guy! I was in *"throwing the money changers out of the temple"* mode and didn't care who knew it.

And then there was the guy who would call the house from prison every so often to talk to Dave. He would remind me that he was the one who had killed his grandmother. Dave was never home to take those calls. I found it a little hard to chat over old times with a murderer.

Someone called the house very late one night. Dave was not home. I had been asleep but woke up completely when the first words out of the guy's mouth were *"Write this down! If your husband does not meet with me in three days, I will bomb your church."*

I wrote it down, although I really didn't have to. It's funny how well you can remember those kinds of threats.

One day the phone rang and the man on the other end of the line confessed to killing five people at one of our local factories. His words were, *"They tried to get me. I got them instead. There are five dead ones at..."* And he named the factory. He didn't leave his name and number.

I didn't have to write those words down either. (By the way, no one was actually killed. I think he was just trying to *"make my day."*)

I have to be honest. I was very grateful when caller ID was invented. It meant I could have some idea of who was calling. I wanted to track down those precious people and pay for their kids' weddings.

You also need a good healthy gift of hospitality to be a pastor's wife. At least you probably should. I don't. It's an effort to open my home to everyone and I do mean everyone.

One night my husband got up to close out the service and invited everyone to our home. What could I make? Pull out five loaves and two fish and look for twelve baskets?

I wasn't a bit spiritual in any of those situations. So every one of these stories points to the fact that I don't have what it takes to be a good pastor's wife.

And I don't have what it takes to be a good person or a good church member or a good Christian or anything else you can attach the word *"good"* to. We aren't good. But He is. And when He lays His heart over mine and He takes my hands and puts them in His and He whispers to me that I am not able but He is, it is enough.

You have no idea how good chocolate covered ice cubes can be!

Luke 9

Luke 9:10 tells us that the disciples returned and reported to Jesus what they had done. I have to wonder what that means. A few verses above tell us that He had sent out the twelve. They had shared the Gospel, healed, taken authority over demons.

I cannot even imagine what that trip was like.

Because He had sent them out, He didn't walk beside them on the dusty roads. He wasn't a few feet ahead stretching out His hands to bring hope and healing to the people. This time He sent them out.

"Take nothing for the journey-" Luke 9:3

They didn't need money, or extra clothes, or even food. They were not to call ahead to make reservations for the night. God would put people in their path who would open their homes, their pantries, and their money bags. They didn't need anything for the trip. So how can you do anything with nothing in your hands?

But it happened. God gave the disciples people who welcomed them. He led them to those who had hearts that would not count the cost. Instead they would count the lives. The results were incredible.

He had given them their mission. They were to preach the Gospel.

They saw a big God. They saw how great.

Healings occurred, demons were cast out, diseases were cured, and they preached the good news. The Bible doesn't give us a number to accompany the results, but we do see that there was something wonderful to report. Their hearts were overflowing. It had been an awesome trip.

They probably felt a chorus of emotions. Were they ecstatic, tired, joyful, fearful, drained, energized, worried that they had not done enough, proud that they had done so much? Were there hearts rejoicing as they walked up to tell Jesus?

We don't know. We do know that when they came back to Jesus, they reported all they had done... hmmm...all they had done.

His response?

He took them to a place where they could be alone.

But when you are making an impact the way Jesus was, you don't stay in the shadows very long.

The crowd heard where He was and followed.

Jesus welcomed them. The results were incredible.

He spoke to them about the Kingdom of God. He cured those who needed healing. But as the day began to wear away, the twelve began to wear down.

They wanted Jesus to send the crowd out. They went to Him and said, *"Send the crowd away…"* Luke 9:12

They wanted the crowd to find their own place to stay, their own food to eat and use their own money bags to do it.

But Jesus had given them their mission. *"You give them something to eat."* Luke 9:13

They saw a big problem. They saw how little!

With only five small loaves of bread and two little fish…they were to feed the crowd.

It gives us a number. There were 5,000 men. We don't know how many women and children.

The disciples counted the cost. How do you feed thousands when you have so little in your hands?

But these disciples were about to be let in on a secret. It doesn't matter how much is in our hands. It matters what is in His. It doesn't matter how large the crowd and how limited our resources.

What matters is what He tells us to do.

Everyone ate until they were satisfied. Everyone had enough.

The disciples were asked to pick up the leftovers.

They picked up twelve baskets full of broken pieces. Were their hearts broken as they bent over to see what was left over from all He had done?

We don't know.

We do know this...

It had been an awesome day.

Day 33

Celebration Day

Psalm 148

"Praise the Lord. Praise the Lord from the heavens; praise Him in the heights above."

As you read Psalm 148 today, exalt the Name of the Lord.

Day 34

"I cannot become a Christian!"

She announced it in broken English. And according to her religion, she couldn't. It would mean leaving her heritage, her culture, her religion, her family. It would mean in the least being ostracized. It could mean death. She knew she could not become a Christian. And yet, she came to the meeting.

We were in a foreign country. We did not speak the language. We were attempting to teach students who understood only a little English.

We needed an interpreter. If you have never taught using a translator, let me just say, it isn't easy. Teachers try to maintain a train of thought. That is difficult enough when the teaching is all in English. But it is very difficult when your train of thought is constantly interrupted after a sentence or two, by what you have just said being translated into another language. This was a first for us, so this was by no means flawless teaching.

Thankfully, we had brought with us a little carton of what looked like ordinary plastic Easter eggs. But contained in each egg was a little surprise that helped to illustrate the Easter story. There was a small donkey to tell about Palm Sunday as Jesus rode into Jerusalem. One contained some coins to tell about Judas' betrayal, another held a piece of purple cloth for Jesus' robe. A small crown of thorns, a cross, a rock, with each egg we could tell a bit of the Easter story. The last was empty so we could tell about the empty tomb, that Jesus had conquered death. We shared the wonderful miracle of Easter.

And then a miracle took place. The love of God, that had crossed the barrier of man's sin, also crossed the language barrier, the barrier of awkward teaching, of religion, of heritage, of culture and entered the heart of a young girl.

"I cannot become a Christian," she said it again, *"but I can have Jesus in my heart!"*

I don't think the Apostle Paul, when he was out arresting Christians, had any intention of becoming a Christian either. And then, for him, a miracle, Paul opened his heart to the Savior. And now, for her, a miracle, she also had opened her heart to Jesus.

Luke 18

He was rich. He was young. He was a ruler. Anything the world had to offer he probably already owned, but if not, his credit cards held no limits. Power, prestige, prominence, defined him. Life was good.

But the question of eternity kept cropping up. Where would he spend it?

So he sought out Jesus, the Rabbi. *"Good Teacher, what must I do to inherit eternal life?"* Luke 18:18

The question was what the young man could DO, so Jesus began there. He said, *"You know the commandments; Do not commit adultery, do not murder, do not steal, do not give false testimony, honor your father and mother."* Luke 18:20

This young ruler said he had kept the law, even from his youth. Do you suppose those words caught in his throat? Had he really kept the law perfectly?

So Jesus helped him to see what was actually in his heart. He told him to sell his possessions and give to the poor, and then to choose the only way to eternal life: Follow Him. Jesus wanted him to stop trusting himself, relying on his own goodness, riches, power, position, and choose the Savior.

But the young man couldn't, he wouldn't. He had too much of the earthly to choose the heavenly, the here and now was more important than the hereafter.

Sadly, he looked into the face of Eternal Life and walked away.

The Bible doesn't tell us if he ever came back. Did he rethink this decision? We hope at some point in his life that He made the choice to follow Christ.

Day 35

A trip to an island in the Bahamas, would we like to go? All expenses paid, did we want it? What would you say? Of course we said, *"Yes!"*

I looked forward to the alone time with my husband, lounging on the beach and sleeping long into the morning. Then I could grab coffee and my Bible to have a quiet time gazing at the azure blue ocean, cloudless blue sky and hearing gentle waves slapping the white sandy beach. Rest, no schedule, no appointments, no commitments, no getting children off to school, this was a dream trip afforded to us by my husband's company.

But at 5:00 AM the next morning my eyes popped open. I could not sleep. Still slightly dark, I felt almost as if I had an appointment in this no appointment place. I grabbed my Bible and headed for the beach right outside our door, an appointment with the Lord. He always shows up. This was more restful than bed rest.

But the next day I thought sure I would just sleep in. But again, wide awake at that 5:00 AM hour, and once again a feeling that I had an appointment. And Jesus was right there waiting. He never disappoints. He always keeps appointments. He met me on that deserted piece of glorious beach that He had created for just such a time as this.

One more day before we headed back to the schedule and this day I was sure I would simply sleep away the morning. But you guessed it. I woke early and yet again was flooded with the feeling that I had a meeting to keep. I went outside to what had become my strip of beach, my sanctuary, my little piece of heaven. I opened my Bible, alone, and yet not alone. Suddenly a shadow fell over me. I looked up and there standing above me on this deserted strip of beach in the twilight of the morning was a huge Bahamian man. His frame completely overshadowed mine.

The man knelt down next to me and said as close as I can remember, these words, *"I want to ask you a question. I see you are reading the Bible and I would like to know something. I am a Christian and I am married, but there is another woman who is interested in me and I am interested in her. Would it be okay to pursue a relationship with her?"*

I do remember my exact words. I looked him square in the face and said with every bit of the firmness that my voice could generate, *"Do not do it! God has sent me here to tell you, DO NOT DO THAT! You will regret it with every fiber of your being."*

And then I knew that God had brought me to this beautiful island as a missionary for that moment. He wanted a message delivered and for some unknown reason picked me to deliver it. I was so humbled, so grateful to have the privilege of being a tool in God's hands. The man's name was Leon. We talked a little more until my husband came looking for me. I still pray for Leon and hope that he made a Godly choice.

I also remind the Lord occasionally that I would be good to go again on an all-expense paid trip to a remote little island as a missionary for a few days. I'm just saying.

Luke 19

Appointments, we all have them. Some have more than others. We see doctors and dentists. We might have work related appointments. Some we look forward to. Some, like colonoscopies, we may literally dread. Some we know way in advance. Some surprise us and turn out to be the kind we never forget.

Zacchaeus heard that Jesus was coming to town. Jericho was about thirty miles from Jerusalem, but news of this One who could heal blind eyes, cast out demons, even raise the dead, news like that spread. And then news of His coming to Jericho spread like wildfire. Everyone wanted to see Him. There would be crowds and crowds of people.

Zacchaeus was a tax collector. He was wealthy. Tax collectors were notorious for cheating people out of more than just their fair share of money. Tax collectors were disliked, even hated in polite circles because they cheated their own kind. Most of the time, they were Jews who worked for the Romans and then exacted exorbitant sums from their fellow Jews. Rich but hated, wealthy, but unwelcome. Yes, gold coins might jingle in his pocket, but his life, like old Ebenezer Scrooge would have been a miserly one.

Zacchaeus heard that Jesus was coming to town.

Now Zacchaeus had a choice. He could have stayed

in bed. He could have stayed at home. He could have stayed in the crowd, but he wanted to see Jesus. So he got up. He went to the place where Jesus would be coming. He left the crowd. He ran to a sycamore fig tree. He climbed high because he wanted to see Jesus.

And you know what? Jesus stopped. Jesus spoke. Jesus came home with Zacchaeus and his life was never the same again.

And what about us? Is there something keeping us from an appointment with the Savior? Is it our bed, staying at home, sitting in the crowd? Are we missing the most important appointment of our lives?

Day 36

I love to paint pottery, clay formed into some lovely bowl or decorative plate. I like to put a lot of detail into it. It takes me forever. I like to sit where there is the most light so I can see what I'm doing. At our local pottery studio the most light is in the front of the store.

On this particular day the studio was filled with children, probably about fifty. There were a few adults. I was just innocently painting pottery. As usual, much detail was on my piece. The children in the studio probably ranged in ages from about eight to ten. A young man about nine years old stopped to ask me about my painting. He had lots of questions. I answered them. He wanted to know colors and why I switched paintbrushes. I've been an art teacher. Here was a young man eager to learn technique. I was glad to answer.

Remember I was in front by the window. All of a sudden from the back of the studio a young girl began to scream at the top of her lungs. She called the young man standing next to me by name, *"DON'T YOU KNOW STRANGER DANGER?"*

You could hear a pin drop.

Stranger danger is serious. We teach our children not to talk to strangers for a reason. Bad things can happen.

So I started looking around for the vile perpetrator.

Then suddenly I realized she was referring to ME as the *"stranger danger"*.

I could feel the redness, the heat, the hot flashes pulsing all the way through me up to my face.

AWKWARD! SO EMBARRASSING! WAIT A MINUTE, I'M A GRANDMOTHER. I AM NO STRANGER DANGER! I HAVE BEEN WRONGLY ACCUSED!

John 9

Clay...it can be used to make decorative pottery. It can be used to make jars, cups, pitchers and plates for everyday use. But 2000 years ago it was used to heal a man. It seems like an odd choice to put dirt, clay dug out of the ground, on someone's eyes since even a little speck of dirt in the eye can cause discomfort. Yet Jesus didn't follow any expected routine. He did what was the right choice for each situation.

Also when we think about dirt, clay, mud, we think about something that is pretty mundane. But let's be reminded that often Jesus used the ordinary to show the extraordinary.

"As He went along, He saw a man blind from birth. His disciples asked Him, 'Rabbi, who sinned, this man or his parents that he was born blind?'" John 9:1-2

This blind man was being accused of sinning so much, even before he was born, that he deserved to be blind forever. Or they were asking if his parents were such wicked sinners that their tiny child should pay for their sins.

It was a common belief that if someone was sick, or hurt, or crippled, it was a natural consequence to their sin. There are consequences to sin. But in this case, *"Neither this man, nor his parents sinned,"* said Jesus, *"but this happened so that the works of God might be displayed in him."* verse 3

This was a different twist. It happened so that God

could display His works. Maybe if we are going through some challenge, some physical infirmity, some trial, we should look to see what work God wants to display through it.

Then Jesus spit on the ground, made some mud and put it on the man's eyes.

This same One who back in the Garden of Eden had taken the dust, the dirt from the ground, and formed it into a man now took that same hand and reached down into the dirt for mud that could be spread over blinded eyes. And the One who created the first man now recreated those eyes that had never seen light, or a sunrise, or his parents' faces, or trees or anything else.

"'Go, He told him, "wash in the Pool of Siloam" (this word means 'Sent') *So the man went and washed, and came home seeing."* John 9:6-7

People were so confused. Was this the blind man? No, he only looks like him. How can he see? How were those eyes opened?

They took him to the Pharisees who questioned this once blind man. They brought in his parents and questioned them. This was beyond their understanding. It was beyond everyone's understanding because it was miraculous and the man testified to that.

More debate, more argument, more anger...they said to the man, *"'You were steeped in sin at birth; how dare you lecture us!' And they threw him out."* verse 34

But yet another sweet encounter with the Savior. And now, not only were this man's physical eyes opened but his spiritual ones as well. *"Then the man said, 'Lord, I believe,' and he worshiped Him."* John 9:38

Born blind and now he could see, not only sunsets, and trees and his parents' faces, but also he could see....Jesus.

Because we are steeped in sin, we are also born blind. Yet the Savior, the Creator of the world wants to heal our blinded eyes so we can join our voices with that of the songwriter...*"I once was blind, but now I see."*

Day 37

"Cancer!"

It was the diagnosis, and for Dad it was terminal. He lived ten months after the diagnosis, and was often sick. He was still young, maybe old in a child's eyes, but still young and vibrant in the eyes of most adults. We prayed, we pleaded, we sent word to Jesus over and over to please come and heal our dad.

And yet, Dad died.

Why didn't God answer our prayers? Why, when we asked and pleaded did He not say *"Yes"* to a healing? We simply did not understand, but were confronted with a choice. Would we choose to trust the heart of God, even if we couldn't see His hand?

The funeral, the burial, all part of the death experience. Dad was the first of ten siblings to die. His funeral was sad, because we knew we would have a very long time to miss him. But it was not the kind of overwhelming grief that can accompany a death, because we had the calm assurance that Dad was in the presence of the Lord. There were tears, but even some laughter. There was grief, but also some rejoicing. The *"whys"* were not answered, but the trust was there.

All six of us have moved away from our Ohio roots,

so we get home rarely. But a family reunion called me back. I talked to lots of aunts and uncles and cousins. One conversation with a cousin began to reveal a change in his life. We had known this kid growing up and knew that he was not interested in the things of God. So what prompted the change? I wanted to know.

"It was at your dad's funeral. I couldn't understand how you could still have joy in the middle of all that. I wanted to know and went on a search. It led me to Jesus."

A reason, a hint of an answer to the *"Why?"* of Dad's death. Dad's death had allowed someone to see he needed Jesus.

That doesn't erase the pain of death, but I'm fairly certain that if we were to ask Dad about it today, he would say it was absolutely worth it. One of these days I'll have that privilege.

John 11

"Now a man named Lazarus was sick. He was from Bethany, the village of Mary and her sister Martha." John11:1

"So the sisters sent word to Jesus, 'Lord, the one you love is sick.'" John 11:3

Lazarus was sick. Lazarus was dying, so the sisters went right to the source of help. They sent word to Jesus.

Verses 5-6 say, *"Now Jesus loved Martha and her sister and Lazarus. So when he heard that Lazarus was sick, He stayed where He was two more days..."*

Wait! Back up, it says He loved them SO he stayed where He was for two more days. He loved them, but He DID NOT COME TO ANSWER THEIR CRY FOR HELP. Jesus waited on purpose. He waited because He loved them.

We read that and it leaves us with questions. Jesus waited and by the time He arrived, Lazarus was already dead.

Martha came to meet Him.

"'Lord,' Martha said to Jesus, 'if You had been here my brother would not have died.'" John 11:21

We can almost hear her question of *"Why"*. We can feel her broken heart.

Mary said the same thing in verse 32, *"Lord, if You had been here my brother would not have died."*

Mary and Martha both knew that Jesus had the power to heal. They absolutely had enough faith that Jesus could heal their brother. This was not lack of faith. It was not because they didn't ask the right way. It was not because they had too much sin in their lives. Jesus did not answer because He loved them.

Yes, Jesus could have healed Lazarus with a touch. He could have healed him with a word. Jesus could have healed him from where He was; Jesus didn't even have to come. But He didn't come right away, He didn't heal Lazarus. Jesus let Lazarus die and by the time He came, he was dead, decaying, stinking in the grave.

How is this love?

This love allowed moments of grief so they could come to see that Jesus was more, that He was bigger.

Mary and Martha already knew beyond a shadow of a doubt that Jesus was the God who Heals, but what they did not yet fully grasp was that He was also the Resurrection and the Life. His power was greater than healing.

"Then Jesus said, "Did I not tell you that if you believe, you will see the glory of God." John 11:40

He called forth Lazarus and in that breathtaking moment, they knew that Jesus is Life itself.

Day 38

All of us have circumstances. They are often used as excuses but they can be used as opportunities. We get to choose.

Our son had to spend some time in a wheel chair. For this story, the circumstances don't matter. What matters is that because Dave had spent a lot of extra time with Josh, he wanted to carve out a special time with our daughter.

She wanted him to go on a day long field trip with her class. He was hoping for an evening out at a restaurant when they could talk over what was going on in her life. She wanted a load of middle school kids crowded onto a bus where she sat with her friends and he sat with the other parent chaperones, exhausted after keeping watch over their field trip of wandering lambs.

Dave has a shepherd's heart but this was not exactly his first choice. He didn't really see this as spending time with our daughter. However, he had left himself wide open and honored her request.

It wasn't his trip. He had no responsibilities on the way home. These were unusual circumstances for him. He could rest a little as the day wound down, night fell, and the bus began the star trek home.

Well, that's what he thought.

Sorry...not on the agenda. After they had been on the bus for a little while, one of the teachers took the seat next to Dave for a few moments.

"I don't think the bus driver is a Christian."

We are to have a relentless pursuit of the things of God. Our days are to be consumed with a white hot passion to take the Gospel wherever we place our feet.

However, being on a day long field trip with a bus load of middle schools kids makes you really tired. He could have used that as an excuse to just stay in his seat. He could have been reluctant to go.

But Dave moved to the front of the bus. He introduced himself, visited about the day and then began to ask some probing questions about the bus driver's relationship with Christ. They talked through the meaning and the way to this new life. The bus driver heard and responded.

Some of the kids saw and heard.

All of the kids understood when one week later they learned that their bus driver had had a heart attack and died.

An eternal difference had taken place on that trip home.

All of us have circumstances. They can be used as excuses or they can be used as opportunities. We get to choose.

The greater purpose for the trip had changed. It wasn't just about spending time with a daughter. It was about an opportunity to share Christ.

John 12

These were the circumstances:

Jesus had raised Lazarus from the dead. Can you imagine? Your brother, your friend, your neighbor, dead and buried for four days and suddenly he is sitting in front of you having dinner. It is no wonder that they were giving a party in Jesus' honor to celebrate life. Nothing had ever happened in their lives, city, history that could rival those circumstances. The victory was overwhelming.

A burial had become preparation for a banquet. Jesus had spoken and life had come.

Brokenness consumed her, but passion ignited her. She could have been reluctant because of her sin, but she was relentless because of her love. No custom, tradition, dignity, would prevent her from pursuit of her mission.

She knelt next to her Savior and spilled her heart through the fragrance of the most precious possession she had. Mary poured out a pint of a perfume that was worth a year's wages. Her words came as tears as she wiped His feet with her hair. The party was startled. Both eyebrows and questions were raised.

One question was verbalized.

"But one of His disciples, Judas Iscariot, who was to betray him, objected, 'Why wasn't this perfume

sold and the money given to the poor? It was worth a year's wages.'" John 12:4-5

Judas had no heart for the poor but he had a heart for the riches.

The anointing had raised questions.

"Leave her alone," Jesus replied. "It was intended that she should save this perfume for the day of my burial. You will always have the poor among you but you will not always have me." John 12:7

Jesus had spoken and death would come.

A burial had become preparation for a banquet. A banquet had now become preparation for a burial.

Day 39

I love seeing talent. And because I am a mom I think my kids have a lot of it. I have always enjoyed seeing them involved in everything. I have laughed, cried, giggled and cheered at their antics. It has almost always been fun to listen to them practice and then see them in action. Once our daughter suffered a concussion, but the next evening still went out on stage to bring the house down. At least we thought she did. So when they have been in the center of anything, we have always been right there rooting them on. From sports to plays and from concerts to art, we have loved it.

But there was one time...

It was the end of our son's fifth grade year. He was popular, pretty self-confident and about as grounded as an almost teenager can be. He was getting good grades, doing his homework and involved in all kinds of church activities.

This was before the teenage years hit hard and someone else moved in to possess his body. But he was actually still fairly normal at that point.

It was a banquet and all of the students and all of their parents were there.

We got settled at the table and dinner was served. Just before the program began we happened to notice the schedule for the evening's entertainment. It was then that we saw our son's name. Next to it were the words *"Trumpet Solo."*

Josh didn't own a trumpet. His dad had one but it was bent and hadn't been played in decades. I knew it hadn't been tuned. And even if Josh had been able to scare up a trumpet, he had never practiced one that I had ever heard.

But there it was. Our son's name and right next to it was *"Trumpet Solo."*

The name of the tune he would be playing wasn't there, and no one to accompany him. He was striking out into the music business on his own. He was feeling pretty good about this. I could see it on his face. There wasn't any time to talk. The program was about to begin.

I watched him as he moved to center stage. I was afraid. He smiled and then he began.

He began, and then he kept going and going and going. It was the longest trumpet solo I had ever heard.

When it was finally over, I whispered to him. *"What was that song?"*

His answer? *"I made it up."*

Somehow I knew that.

Luke 19

"The Lord needs it."

Two of the disciples were sent. *"As they were untying the colt, its owners asked them, 'Why are you untying the colt?'*

They replied, 'The Lord needs it.'" Luke 19:33-34

Such a simple answer, such a powerful answer and the owners let go of what was theirs because the Lord needed it.

Cloaks were spread over it and Jesus rode this animal into Jerusalem. It was the tenth day of Nisan. It was a Sunday. It has become known as Palm Sunday.

People gathered. They began to throw their cloaks down on the ground to make a path for Jesus. They began to shout. They were praising God for the miracles they had seen and oh what miracles there had been.

Blind eyes were opened and for the very first time those eyes could see. People crippled from birth were walking among them. Demons had been cast out and peace had entered into the hearts of those who had once been possessed. Lazarus had been raised from the dead. Yes, there was so much to celebrate. For here, in their midst was the One who had touched and spoken healing and life.

"Blessed is the King who comes in the name of the Lord! Peace in heaven and glory in the highest."
Luke 19:38

"Hosanna", save us, was lifted from their hearts and shouted with their voices. SAVE US...for that is what *'hosanna'* means. The cry was for this King to release them from the bondage of Roman rule.

Palm branches were raised and waved as Jesus rode past.

The Pharisees in the crowd said to Jesus, "Teacher, rebuke your disciples!" "I tell you," He replied, "if they keep quiet, the stones will cry out."
Luke 19:39-40

Jesus knew that the praise had to burst forth. It was literally waiting at the surface of the earth to be raised. If the people had not been shouting and praising Jesus, the King of Kings and the Lord of Lords, the very rocks He had created would have lifted their voices in a chorus of exaltation.

But He also knew that this praise would not be lasting. He knew what He was riding into Jerusalem to do. Ahead of Him that week, He could see the torture, He could see the cross, He could see the sin that He was going to bear and His heart broke.

As He approached Jerusalem and saw the city, He wept over it and said, *"If you, even you, had only known on this day what would bring you peace— but now it is hidden from your eyes."* Luke 19:42

They wanted a king who would release them from their bondage. *"Hosanna"* would turn into *"Crucify."*

What they didn't know was that this was going to be the ultimate salvation, freedom from the bondage of sin and death.

"Hosanna, Lord, save us," and with His death, He made that salvation possible.

Day 40

Celebration Day

Psalm 149, Psalm 113-118, Luke 19

"Praise the Lord. Sing to the Lord a new song,
His praise in the assembly of His faithful people."

Today is Palm Sunday. So as you lift your hallelujahs and praises you might want to read a little more. Read Psalm 149, Psalms 113-118 (This is called the Hallel. It is where we get the word hallelujah. These Psalms are read during the Passover season.) Also turn to the account in Luke 19 of Jesus riding into Jerusalem.

It is such a great day to praise the Lord, and if we don't do it, the rocks will cry out.

Day 41

What do bowling balls and Harley-Davidson®
motorcycles have to do with each other? Don't know?
Actually I guess I appear to be the link. I've told you
that I'm single. Born into a group of three, raised in a
family of eight, I was the first one married. So I went
from being part of a group to being part of a couple.
Being divorced then at age 50, it was the very first
time I had been single. Getting used to that has been
a real challenge. I had to try to find my own identity.
It really is wonderful that God has an identity for me
because the way other people see me is sometimes
a little hard to wrap my mind around. (If you read
Catch Your Breath...you might remember the guy
who wanted to reinvent me...ahhh good times.)

But here's another example. I changed my hairstyle.
A woman at church came up and complimented
me...well sort of. She said, *"Oh, I'm so glad you've
done something about your hair. We've been praying
about that."*

Praying about my hair....I had to wonder who the
"WE" in that sentence was ...Her family? The Ladies
Sunday School Class? The whole church? I didn't
ask. I managed to gulp out *"Well, we know that
God has our hairs all numbered so I guess He's
concerned about it too."*

Then as a newly single person the first two times someone asked me for a date I was invited to go bowling. I turned both men down. I wasn't ready to yet date...I still pretty much feel that way most of the time. But I had to take a look at myself and ask what it was about me that seemed to say, *"I would love to go to a smoky, noisy, gym-like atmosphere, where I put on other people's sweaty shoes and throw a ball down into a gutter?"*

Recently a man walked up to me at school. He's been a substitute where I work. Now, I am the instructional coach in my building. I work mostly with students who have reading deficiencies to try to bridge those gaps. I also look at data and work with teachers. When there's a substitute in the building, I try to meet the person and help in any way I can to make their day go smoothly. This man has been in our building frequently this year so he knows who I am. I usually try to check in to see how things are going.

In the gym for morning assembly, he walked up to me. *"I'm going to buy you something."* he said.

My response was *"What? Why are you buying me something?"*

He replied, *"Well, I just think you need it."*

"What do you think I need?" I was thinking that he

~ *213* ~

thought I needed some type of school related item.

He said, *"I'm going to buy you a Harley-Davidson shirt"*

"What? Why on earth would you want to buy me that?"

"I just think it fits you."

Are you kidding me? *"A Harley-Davidson shirt? No! I don't need that."*

Now I honestly wasn't trying to be rude, but I was stunned. I don't know the man very well. Secondly I couldn't fathom why Harley-Davidson and my name would even remotely come up together in the same sentence. I perceive myself as usually sporting a more tailored look, you know a jacket with a nice pair of slacks. (I have been known to even choose a skirt with a lovely green leafy pattern.)

"I teach Bible classes, Sunday school...I'm not a Harley rider."

He said, *"If I buy it for you, will you wear it?"*

My response? *"I cannot even imagine going to my closet in the morning and pulling out a biker shirt and thinking 'Oh this looks like a good outfit for the day'."*

I made it pretty clear that that would never be a

wardrobe choice I would make. But I did ask him, *"Why would you even think that fits me?"* He said, *"Because you are so tough."*

Okay, he did have that right. Often when there are subs in the rooms, kids believe it's a great time for recess all day. They look over the situation and say, *"Hmmm, he doesn't know how things are supposed to go so we can do whatever we want."*

When I walk into the classroom, they know I know the rules and I know what happens when the rules are broken. So immediately things calm down when I come in. My presence helps to get things back on track.

As I said earlier, it is God who has established who I am. It is His identity that I want to represent. I don't do it well, I have often misrepresented Him, but I want Him to be seen in and through my life. This is what I know. Jesus was tough. Others tried to superimpose their identity on Him. They wanted Him to fit the mold that they perceived. He did not. He was not afraid to address what was wrong. When He walked in, His presence changed the room.

So I guess if I am perceived as tough enough to wear biker gear and bowling shoes, then so be it.

Luke 19

Passover was a sacred time. It was a time for cleansing and making sure that all of the leaven was gone from the household. It is where the idea of spring cleaning comes from. Every room, every space, every corner was to be swept clean. Leaven is any type of agent that makes food rise such as yeast, or bread starter, baking powder or soda. According to the Bible, it represents sin. It was a picture for them and is a picture for us to get rid of sin.

It was almost Passover and there was a great deal of activity going on at the Temple when Jesus approached. Sheep, doves, cattle and people were milling around. Men had set up tables and were selling.

When Jesus showed up everything changed.

We would not have been able to understand exactly what their motives were on that day. They were cheating the people, but maybe they were also so focused on the bottom line of the shekel that they were robbing God of the prayer, worship and praise that He deserved. Jesus knew their motives. He saw their hearts.

Luke 19:45-46 *"When Jesus entered the temple courts, He began to drive out those who were selling. 'It is written,' He said to them, 'My house shall be called a house of prayer but you have made it a den of robbers.'"*

Jesus could see their intent. He could see the larceny in their hearts. They had turned this place that was supposed to be a place of prayer and worship, into a place of thievery. Jesus was angry and rightly so. Mark 11 tells us He overturned the tables of the money changers and the benches of those selling doves and the Scripture also tells us He made a whip to do it. He cleansed the Temple and just like the preparation for the Passover, He was getting rid of the leaven, the sin.

For years the people had practiced the cleansing of their homes. Now, here was the picture that God had given them way back in Egypt, being played out right before their eyes.

So did they see it? They should have. Psalm 69:9 told them that the One who would come would be consumed with zeal for the house of God.

Yes, they should have known. But they didn't. Instead, they looked for a way to destroy Him.

Luke 19:47 *"Every day He was teaching at the temple. But the chief priests, the teachers of the law and the leaders among the people were trying to kill Him."*

Their goal was to kill this spotless lamb and Passover was coming.

Day 42

Surprises.

I didn't see him. No one did. But apparently he thought that life at my home was better than hiding out under a porch. So he decided to hitch a ride with us.

Who was our stow-a-way?

Not a beautiful white Persian kitten. It was not a sweet little Husky puppy. I might have been okay with a not quite grown Irish Setter or miniature Collie.

But what put himself into the back of our van to travel the two hours home?

A carsick, one-eyed, black cat.

I have had other animals in my life. I came home one day and ran upstairs to change clothes and there sitting on my bed was our cat. She was a full grown charcoal feline completely content on my bed.

Here is the problem: I DON'T OWN A CAT!

Another day I was working in my kitchen when something streaked passed me. It was big and black and hairy. We had a dog at that time but she was not coal colored and certainly not that big. This was a mammoth dark poodle that thought there was a party at my house. I had a choice. I could either gather my wits and send him home without his party hat or hand him the phone to dial 911 because I was in the fetal position.

I had to chase a cat off of our school bus in order to let my students board for a field trip.

We caught a mink in our yard.

I have been in a car surrounded by buffalo. I've heard elk bellow. I've watched a coyote with his kill.

I stared a grizzly in the face and as I ran for the car someone shouted *"Don't run!"*

Sure!

I didn't see any of this coming. I would have been better prepared if I had known, but there was no heads-up. No warning. No neon sign that flashed animal crossing. Well, there was a sign about the buffalo and elk but not until we were right there.

And that is really okay. Everyone has little moments when life catches you by surprise.

But the most significant events in all of history were not meant to come as a surprise. They had been spoken over and over, but it seems that almost no one was listening.

Luke 20

Jesus had ridden into Jerusalem. For the next few days He was teaching. For the next few days the religious leaders were trying to trap Him.

"One day as Jesus was teaching the people in the temple courts and proclaiming the good news, the chief priests and the teachers of the law came to him." Luke 20:1

They came with questions and every time, they thought they had such a hard question that He would stumble and say the wrong thing.

"Tell us by what authority you are doing these things, they said. Who gave you this authority?" Luke 20:2

Jesus could see right through the question. He wasn't one bit intimidated. He wasn't worried about what He should say next. Jesus answered them with a question, *"Tell me: John's baptism-was it from heaven or of human origin?"* Luke 20:3

Well, now the tables were turned. They knew they were in a no-win situation. If they said from heaven, Jesus would ask them why they didn't believe John, and if they said of human origin the people would have stoned them. *"So they answered, 'We don't know where it was from.'*

Jesus said, 'Neither will I tell you by what authority I am doing these things.'" Luke 20:7-8

Then they sent spies, pretending to be sincere. Again, they just wanted to catch him. This time they hoped He would say something against Caesar and they could hand Him over to the authorities.

This would be a great question.

"Teacher we know that you speak and teach what is right, and that you do not show partiality but teach the way of God in accordance with the truth. Is it right for us to pay taxes to Caesar or not?" Luke 20:21-22

So they had Him...there was no way He could get this question right. He couldn't go against Caesar, but on the other hand the Jewish people hated being under Roman rule. This was the perfect question.

But they didn't bargain on the fact that the One they were questioning was the very One who had formed them in their mother's wombs. He didn't just know the answers, He was the answer.

"He saw through their duplicity and said to them, 'Show me a denarius. Whose image and inscription are on it?'

'Caesar's,' they replied"

So simple...

"Then give back to Caesar what is Caesar's and to God what is God's.'" Luke 20:23-25

They couldn't trap Him. When questioned, Jesus always answered perfectly.

So why didn't they realize who He was? He answered every challenge. He did miracle after miracle. Blind eyes were opened, lepers were healed, people were raised from the dead. Yet these religious leaders did not see it. They were completely caught off guard.

Jesus had been prophesied. Daniel, Isaiah, Psalms, all throughout the entire Scripture, the Messiah was identified, but they missed it. They missed Him.

Why?

Because they were not looking.

So what about us? Are we looking?

Day 43

I have to agree with Kris. Medical procedures are not fun. Some stuff you have to do because there are some unknown pains or weird rash or strange warts that are doubling you over or eating your flesh or taking over your body. But some stuff is just routine maintenance. Either way, not eating, only drinking things that somebody cooked up with a chemistry set, and being poked and prodded with needles and torture devices rank pretty low on how I want to spend a day.

But I had to go for the second appointment in a week. I completed the first. That was for an upper GI. Drink Barium for this. Barium? This seems like a drink that should be more akin to nuclear waste than something I put into my mouth and swallow, but when a nurse is standing there with the glass of stuff saying, *"Now drink it all"*, you just do it. I did. Upper GI showed nothing. That was good news, I guess, but what it meant was that in a week I had to come back for the lower G I. And that one required a prep.

The first time a doctor said the word *"prep"* to me I was okay with it because I didn't fully comprehend the scope of what was required. After a few of these over the years I have grown to HATE that word *"prep"*. It usually means some vile hogwash that often comes in a gallon container. A GALLON

CONTAINER OF LIQUID...talk about a great meal! I say meal because it's usually the only thing you are allowed to ingest. Honestly though, when you're drinking it, you have no appetite for anything else. It does something to your taste buds and makes anything else taste just like the horrible concoction.

I dutifully did the prep, chugging down as much of it as I possibly could and later experiencing all the wonders that accompany it. So off to the hospital where the second procedure was to take place. After a bit of checking, I was told that I needed to have yet more prep. This one did not involve drinking and yet liquid still had to make its way inside of me. Then I was told to wait while that prep worked. In the *"holding"* area, dressed in hospital gown and robe, I waited until the magic could happen and I would be completely prepped for the lower GI.

So I sat there in that waiting room with a few other fortunate recipients of the prep. I'm not sure what happened. As I was waiting I could feel myself slipping into darkness. The floor was coming up to meet my eyes or maybe my eyes were going down to meet the floor. I don't know because what I remember next was being carried by a very large orderly to another room and people yelling at me to wake up. I'm pretty sure I did not *"hold"* onto the liquid long enough. You kind of lose concentration when you are passed out cold. I was a mess. Custodians had to be called in. Nurses were added. They may have had to toss the chair I had been sitting in. (What was the hospital staff thinking putting me into a cloth chair?) I had to be completely cleaned up. I kept apologizing to the orderly and everyone else. It was humiliating. I was completely embarrassed. I wanted to get my clothes on and just leave. I never wanted to see these people ever again. But I couldn't leave. There was that other test that I had to have done.

After showering and getting into a clean gown and robe they did an X-ray. The tech guy looked at it and said. *"You haven't gotten rid of all the barium from last week."*

I didn't? I did everything they told me to do. How was I supposed to get rid of the barium?

"We can't do the lower GI today. You'll have to come back next week. We'll give you a prescription for another prep."

Whaaaat? I have to come back here? With these same people?

I hate medical procedures!

Yes, this was humiliating but it was nothing compared to the humiliation that our Savior went through. And He did it for me, for us.

John 13, Luke 22

It was the night to celebrate Passover. The custom was that a slave, the lowliest one in the household, would wash their feet. It was a disgusting, humiliating job. The streets were so dirty. Animals strolled down the road leaving evidence behind. Human waste from inside houses was removed to the outside and tossed into the dust wherever it was convenient. Garbage, rotting food, all was left in the road. There was not garbage pick-up or a sanitation department to cleanse the streets of Jerusalem, so their feet were filthy.

On this night there was no slave among them to wash their feet. And yet Judas, at that very moment, had thirty pieces of silver jingling in his money bag. He had sold out Jesus. Thirty pieces of silver was the very same price for a male slave.

Jesus knelt to wash their feet.

"He came to Simon Peter, who said to Him, 'Lord, are you going to wash my feet?'
Jesus replied, "You do not realize now what I am doing, but later you will understand.'
'No,' said Peter, 'You will never wash my feet.'
Jesus answered, 'Unless I wash you, you have no part with me.'
'Then, Lord,' Simon Peter replied, 'not just my feet but my hands and my head as well!'"
John 13:6-8

Jesus knew the betrayer was among them. He knew Peter would deny Him. He knew the others would scatter. Yet, Jesus bent before each of them to wash their filthy, dirty feet. What service! What humility! What love!

And then the meal. At a Passover meal, this question is asked, *"Why is this night different from all other nights?"*

The story from Exodus is retold:

It was the miracle night of the redemption of God's people, the Exodus from Egypt. Pharaoh had promised deliverance, but then hardened his heart.

The wrath of God was poured out in plagues and then a final one that would ensure their freedom. For the tenth plague, God told them to kill the lamb, put the blood on the doorframes of the homes, and the angel of death would pass over.

The Passover Lamb had to be a year old male, in the prime of life, pure, spotless. Chosen on the tenth day of Nisan, the father brought the lamb into the house to be examined for four days, to make sure it was without blemish. Then it was killed on the fourteenth. How difficult that would have been. After four days, this lamb would have seemed like a part of the family, but freedom came at a price, the life of a lamb.

On Passover the lamb's blood was smeared on the top

and two sides of the doorframe of the home. None of its bones were broken. It was roasted over the fire. Everyone in the household was to take and eat.

In Egypt with no lamb's blood covering over the door frames in the Egyptian homes, each family awoke to shock, grief, and the death of the firstborn son.

Pharaoh told the Children of Israel to leave. God had set them free from the bondage of slavery.

Jesus, in the prime of life, rode into Jerusalem on a donkey. It was the tenth day of Nisan. He went to His Father's House, the Temple. Over the next four days, He was examined, questioned, and finally declared by Pilate to be without spot or blemish, *"I find in Him no fault at all."* John 18:38 KJV

That night as Jesus ate with them, He explained the significance of the meal.

"And He took bread, gave thanks and broke it, and gave it to them, saying, 'This is my body given for you; do this in remembrance of me.'

In the same way, after the supper he took the cup, saying, 'This cup is the new covenant in my blood, which is poured out for you.'" Luke 22:19-20

Everyone was to take and eat.

With the meal done, Jesus went to pray. He wrestled with what was before Him.

In the Garden of Gethsemane, He asked that the cup be taken from Him, the cup of the wrath of God that would be poured out against sin. Every sin, from every person, for all time, would be laid on Jesus, and He would pay the price for it. The weight was great, the anguish was great. Little droplets of blood-filled sweat spilled from His brow as he prayed.

Why was this night different from all other nights?

The story from Exodus was being lived out...the death of the perfect Lamb for the miracle of the redemption of the world. The life of God would be given to set us free from the bondage of sin.

Throughout the Scripture God had been showing them what was to come.

In Genesis 22, just as Abraham was about to sacrifice Isaac, God told him to stop and Abraham killed a ram in Isaac's place.

God used that lamb to set Isaac free.

In the book of Exodus, when the children of Israel were slaves in Egypt, God said to kill a pure, spotless lamb and put the blood on the doorframes of their homes.

This time God used the blood of those lambs to set a nation free.

Then another Lamb...this Lamb was born in a

stable, just like other lambs. Shepherds came to attend Him, just like other lambs. When John the Baptist saw Him, he identified Him as the Lamb of God, who would take away the sin of the world.

Jesus, the perfect, spotless, Lamb of God, would be the ultimate sacrifice.

God would use His death to set the world free.

Day 44

"Take a deep breath, Mother...it's heaven." Those were the last words we spoke to Mom as she took her final breath. She had opened her eyes really wide for just a few moments. Her eyes had been closed for several days. I turned around to see if I could catch a glimpse of what it was she was seeing. I couldn't. For her it was a glorious vision. For us it was death.

Now there was a new reality. We have known our mother every single day of our lives. Death is a rude awakening that smacks you in the face over and over again.

"I need to call Mom and tell her...oh no wait, she is not here."

"Mom's going to make her special dressing for Easter...no, she's gone."

And the pain shoots through you. The reality of the death hits you again and again.

The funeral was preplanned so we did not have to attend to any of the terrible details that are associated with that. There was no casket to choose. She had already done it. It was all selected, even down to the music and that was a gift.

She had lived in Southern Indiana the last twenty-two years of her life, where most of us reside. But our Dad was buried in Robertsville, Ohio, so that is where Mother was to be buried as well.

The visitation on Thursday, the funeral on Friday, a nine hour trip, and then a grave side service on Saturday in Ohio.

Death is terribly sad. The grieving is grueling, exhausting.

We left our dear, sweet mother's body in Ohio.

But that is not where we left our mother. You see she was already in the presence of the Savior. Mom's death meant she crossed from death into life because of another death...death on a cross.

Psalm 22, Matthew 26, 27

With a kiss, Judas, the betrayer, had arranged the arrest. Jesus was taken away and brought before Caiaphas, the high priest. Peter followed at a distance and within a few short hours spewed out his denial three times.

Before the Sanhedrin, Jesus was questioned but Isaiah had prophesied that *"as a sheep before its shearers is silent, He did not open His mouth."* Isaiah 53:7

He was silent until Caiaphas made a demand.

"But Jesus remained silent. The high priest said to Him, 'I charge you under oath by the living God: Tell us if you are the Messiah, the Son of God.'You have said so,' Jesus replied, 'But I say to all of you; From now on you will see the Son of Man sitting at the right hand of the Mighty One and coming on the clouds of heaven.'" Matthew 26:63-64

The high priest tore his clothes; he was so incensed. The rest of them pronounced Jesus worthy of death. They spit on Him, struck Him with their fists, and slapped Him. Throughout the night He was questioned, beaten so severely that you could not tell He was a man, flogged until his flesh hung in strips from his body, His forehead punctured by thorns, covered by a scarlet robe and mocked, and finally He was made to stand before Pilate.

Pilate could not find fault. He pronounced that He was innocent, but the riotous people clamored for more blood, for His death, His death on a cross. And Pilate, after washing his hands, acquiesced.

Jesus, the spotless, innocent Lamb of God stumbled to Calvary with a wooden cross beam across His bare bleeding back.

A mallet smashed the nails deep through the flesh of His hands and feet, affixing Him to the wood. The cross was lifted and dropped into the hole, jarring, tearing every muscle, every tendon.

Centuries before crucifixion was even invented this had been prophesied:

Psalm 22:16-17 *"Dogs surround me, a pack of villains encircles me; they pierce my hands and my feet. All my bones are on display; people stare and gloat over me. They divide my clothes among them and cast lots for my garment."*

Every breath was torture as He pushed His heel against that wooden cross to lift His body enough to fill His lungs. But this was the fulfillment of the first Messianic prophecy told to the serpent way back in Genesis 3:15 *"And I will put enmity between you and the woman and between your offspring and hers; He will crush your head and you will strike His heel."*

And the sin, every sin that had ever been done,

from the eating of the fruit, to the sin of those hurling the insults and pounding the nails, to the sin that would be done by you and me and everyone yet to come, was laid on Jesus just as it said in Isaiah 53:6, *"All we like sheep have gone astray, each of us has turned to our own way; and the Lord has laid on Him the iniquity of us all."*

Is it any wonder He cried out, *"'Eli, Eli, lema sabachthani' (which means 'My God my God why have you forsaken me?')"* Matthew 27:46, Psalm 22:1

Every breath, every word was torture and yet, on that cross He spoke to provide for His mother. On that cross He forgave the thief, and on that cross He asked His Father to forgive those who were the executioners and scoffers.

Again in Psalm 22:15 the prophecy, *"I am poured out like water, and my bones are out of joint. My heart has turned to wax; it has melted within me. My mouth is dried up like a potsherd and my tongue is stuck to the roof of my mouth...."*

And the fulfillment:

John 19:28-31 *"Later, knowing that everything had now been finished, and so that Scripture would be fulfilled, Jesus said, 'I am thirsty.' A jar of wine vinegar was there so they soaked a sponge in it, put the sponge on a stalk of the hyssop plant, and lifted it to Jesus' lips. When He had received the drink, Jesus said, 'It is finished.' With that, He bowed His head and gave up His spirit."*

"It is finished." These are some of the sweetest words ever spoken. Because Jesus fulfilled everything that had to be done, the work was completed, the debt, your debt, my debt, was paid in full.

Passover...and The Lamb of God was sacrificed, the Lamb of God was dead.

Day 45

Watkin Roberts...never heard of him? It's no wonder, he lived most of his life in the shadows.

It was 1910 and this Welch man, with a heart to reach people for Christ, had a dream of seeing the tribal people in India come to know the Savior.

A woman had given him five British pounds with instructions to use it to share the Gospel. He took the money and printed Gospels of John in an Indian dialect that he hoped the people could read. He sent them to the chiefs of some of the village tribes and he waited. What would God do with this seed?

The chief of the Hmar tribe received this little book but couldn't understand it all because it was not his dialect. He sent a messenger to find Mr. Roberts with an appeal. *"Please come and explain it to us."*

Watkin Roberts wanted to go, but India was under British authority and the leadership saw only the danger. *"The Hmar people are fierce headhunters. They kill their enemies and display their heads as trophies. Do not go."*

But Watkin had not only read the hand written appeal from this tribal leader, he felt it deep inside of him. It was a call from God. It was like the Macedonian calling for Paul to come. Watkin

Roberts understood that God wanted these headhunters' hearts. Mr. Roberts offered to pay a year's worth of schooling for some young men if they would go with him to ensure his safe travel there and back.

Did you catch that he was going to share with headhunters who killed their enemies?

The young men did go with him, but he had no suitcases filled with materials written in the Hmar language. With a Gospel of John and a willing heart to share, Watkin Roberts went.

So how could he break through the language barrier? How could he make them understand?

And then a custom...when two tribes agreed to share a boundary in peace, an animal was sacrificed. There on the boundary line, the animal would be slain and the blood would run on both sides, binding the two together.

He now had a way to explain. A death, an animal sacrifice, the blood of the animal to unite the two tribes in peace.

Jesus Christ was the sacrificial Lamb. His death, His shed blood on the boundary line of the cross could bring salvation and peace to anyone who accepted Him. Jesus came to join God and man.

Mr. Roberts told the remarkable story of Jesus and

five young men from that tribal group received Him as Savior and Lord.

Five converts was thrilling. But he wanted to see others come to Christ and Watkin's heart was to not only lead these people to the Lord, he also wanted to disciple them, so they could become leaders.

The mission board had other ideas. The board moved him away from the Hmar people. After that he had only intermittent contact with this small group of believers. Eventually he was forced to leave India altogether because the mission board pulled their support. Watkin Roberts had to borrow money from a Hindu businessman to get home.

What had gone wrong? He had felt so sure that God had sent him. But only five converts, was that to be the extent of his life's work?

He had dreamed of going to India, of being a missionary who saw many lives changed. Now the dream was dead.

Defeat. He moved back to Wales and eventually to Canada.

Yes, the dream, the mission was dead.

John 19, Matthew 27

Jesus was dead.

The dream was dead. The mission was over. The promise of a new kingdom was now out of reach.

Jesus Christ, the Messiah, the Savior of the world, was dead.

Unreality was reality. The grief of His death was overpowering.

Jesus, the One who with a word could calm storms, the One who when He spit on the dirt, He could take mud and open blinded eyes, the One who with a touch could change oozing, unclean, leprous skin and make it clean, the One who could cast a legion of demons out of a wild man and make him whole, the One who spoke life into the dead, was now Himself, dead.

Yes, the mission was over. How could this be? For three and a half years they had given themselves to follow Jesus.

It was over, He was dead, the stark reality...He needed to be buried.

"Later, Joseph of Arimathea asked Pilate for the body of Jesus. Now Joseph was a disciple of Jesus, but secretly because he feared the Jewish leaders. With Pilate's permission, he came and took the

body away. He was accompanied by Nicodemus, the man who earlier had visited Jesus at night. Nicodemus brought a mixture of myrrh and aloes, about seventy-five pounds. Taking Jesus' body, the two of them wrapped it, with the spices, in strips of linen." John 19:38-40

At His birth He was wrapped in strips of cloth and laid in a borrowed manger. At His death He was wrapped in strips of cloth and laid in a borrowed tomb.

At His birth the Magi, wise men from the East, brought myrrh and laid it at His feet. At His death Joseph and Nicodemus brought myrrh and wrapped His body in it.

His birth brought rejoicing. His death brought grieving.

Matthew 27:59-60 tells us *"Joseph took the body, wrapped it in a clean linen cloth, and placed it in his own new tomb that he had cut out of the rock. He rolled a big stone in front of the entrance to the tomb and went away."*

Jesus was dead.

Day 46

Watkin Roberts thought the dream was dead. He couldn't have been more wrong.

A Gospel of John and a heart that was willing to go wherever God would lead....seeds planted.

What grew?

Remember there were five converts. One of them was Chawnga Pudaite and Rochunga is his son. When he was still a child, only ten years old, Rochunga became a believer in Christ. He and his father both felt that he was the one from the village who needed to attend the school almost a hundred miles away so he could learn English. They wanted to create a written version of the Hmar language and translate the Bible into it. So at age ten he walked the ninety-six miles across the Indian jungle alone. This jungle was ravaged with man-eating tigers and pythons, but it was the only way to the school. Four times a year he crossed that jungle. Rochunga studied for years. He worked. He learned. Finally the New Testament was finished.

Now he could send Bibles to his people.

But Rochunga Pudaite's vision was not just for the Hmar people of India. He wanted all of India to receive the Gospel. Dr. Pudaite has formed an organization called Bibles For The World (www.bftw.org) which has at its heart the mission of sending Bibles around the globe. His first project was to send a Bible to every telephone subscriber in India.

Because Watkin Roberts had first heard the call from God to go to India during the Great Welsh Revival, Dr. Pudaite sent one hundred thousand Bibles to Wales in preparation for the 100th anniversary of that revival.

But the mission continued to grow. To date over twenty-two million Bibles have been placed in over 110 countries.

And the goal is even bigger.

The dream is even bigger.

It had begun with a heart to go. Then one woman gave five British pounds. Gospels of John were printed and sent. Watkin Roberts went. Five Hmar headhunters came to Christ. A dream of reaching India was birthed. But then the order for Mr. Roberts to return home was given.

He thought the dream was dead.

He had no idea.

He thought it was little. It was not. It was HUGE.

Today there are about 150,000 Hmar people and 98% of them are believers in Christ.

And the dream continues to grow.

It is referred to as The Billion Bible Dream...a Bible placed in every household on the planet.

What Watkin Roberts did not see was that it would go from one to five to thousands to millions and maybe someday a billion Bibles around the world.

Defeat?
Absolutely not!
VICTORY!

Luke 23

"The women who had come with Jesus from Galilee followed Joseph and saw the tomb and how His body was laid in it. Then they went home and prepared spices and perfumes. But they rested on the Sabbath in obedience to the commandment."
Luke 23:55-56

It was a morning of brokenness. A day of hopelessness stretched before them. These women had watched as their Lord had taken His last breath and was taken down from the cross. Hastily He had been placed in a borrowed tomb before the Sabbath began. Now it was Sunday and they went to attend to His dead body with the only gift they knew. They carried death spices to the grave.

They walked before any light broke into dawn but that didn't matter at all. Their Light was gone.

They didn't know how they would be able to enter the tomb. A stone stood in the way of their final gift to their Master. They didn't know what they would do. As they headed that way, they didn't have any answers at all.

Their Way was gone.

And it had all happened so quickly.

One week before, the city of Jerusalem had been alive with the shouts of *"Hosanna! Blessed is He who comes in the name of the Lord."* Jesus had just entered the city riding on a colt. People had picked up palm branches to hail Him as their leader. They had taken off their cloaks and placed them on the path to declare He was their Lord.

There was joy in the streets. There was celebration in their hearts. The King had come and their voices of praise lifted beyond the confines of the heavens into the chorus of eternity.

This was a day like no other...no ordinary day because this was no ordinary King. The King of Kings was entering the city and the city proclaimed it.

It had to be proclaimed. Before time began, the Word was given that this would be the moment when Jesus would enter Jerusalem. He would be praised!

Yes, there were those who opposed this proclamation. They wanted to still the voices and end the celebration. But if the peoples' voices of praise had been silenced, the rocks would have lifted theirs. His royalty would be announced. Every pebble and boulder would have shouted.

"He is God Almighty" and every stone knew it. If there had been no voices, the rocks would not have stayed quiet for very long.

But soon the joy and praise grew silent. This worship service ended. The people walked away leaving their palm branches in the dust.

Within a few days He was no longer considered a King. He was considered a criminal. They no longer wanted Him to wear royal robes. They wanted Him stripped. They had called for a coronation but now crowned His head with thorns. He was arrested, mocked, abused, whipped. By the time the torture was ended the flesh on His back hung like ribbons, blood oozed and dripped. It was being poured out onto the sand. His face was mangled and swollen. His eyes of love and compassion could no longer be seen. He no longer even resembled a man.

The screams for His crucifixion ripped open the heavens and thundered through eternity.

A cross was mounted on His shoulders as the sins of all mankind for all time were mounted on His back. Nails pierced His hands and feet. The cross was lifted and dropped into a hole in the rock. It stood on the top of the place of the skull. Death swallowed up the Light.

Darkness descended. His last words ended. He breathed the rattle of death. It was over.

The watching world thought His voice had been silenced forever.

They couldn't have been more wrong.

As the women reached the tomb their grief gave way. The stone had been moved. His body was gone and even this last moment of worship had been stolen from them. The death spices still in hand, their death grief still in their hearts.

But then suddenly...

Day 47

Celebration Day, Resurrection Day

Luke 24, Psalm 150

The earth moved and nothing would ever be the same. Two men in robes that gleamed like lightning spoke eternity jarring words. *"Why do you look for the living among the dead? He is not here, He has risen!"* Luke 24:5b-6a

When the rock had been rolled away, life took over and death was left in the grave clothes.

One sin had brought the power of death over the world. It meant that life would end in death.

One death had brought the power of life over the world. It meant that death would end in Life.

When Jesus had breathed His last breath, the world thought it was over. They didn't understand that it was finished!

When He pronounced those words *"It is finished"*, He was not declaring His life to be over. He was declaring our death to be over.

Sin was conquered. The debt was paid.

What the women found was not a dead body.
What they witnessed was an empty tomb.
What they heard was *"He is not here, He has risen!"*
What they knew was that He was alive!
They went to weep. They left in joy.
They went because He was dead. They left because
He is alive.
What they experienced was the miraculous.
They ran to tell.

When that stone had been sealed at the entrance of
the tomb, it uttered defeat.

When that stone had been rolled away, it shouted
victory! It could hold its breath no longer.

The Resurrection! It's breathtaking!

*"Let everything that has breath praise the Lord.
Praise the Lord."* Psalm 150:6

Learn More

Learn more, explore additional writings,
and contact K.L. Kandel at **www.klkandel.com**.

Made in the USA
Charleston, SC
27 January 2017